# Reminiscences of Eighty Years

JOHN URIE.

*Frontispiece.*

# Reminiscences of Eighty Years

## By John Urie

**With Illustrations**

PAISLEY : ALEXANDER GARDNER
Publisher by Appointment to the late Queen Victoria

1908

LONDON:
SIMPKIN, MARSHALL, HAMILTON, KENT & CO., LMD.

PRINTED BY ALEXANDER GARDNER, PAISLEY

# PREFACE.

THIS little volume of Reminiscences has been sent out to the public in response to the wishes of numerous friends. I make no claims for it beyond this, and it represents the recollections of one who has seen many stirring events and met many notable personages of a past generation, that to me at least seems not less interesting or important than the present. The recalling of these incidents, which I can do most readily though now nearing ninety, has been to me a labour of love, and I trust that in this volume will be found much to interest.

I desire to acknowledge the assistance I have received from Mr. James Reid in the preparation of these Reminiscences for the press.

JOHN URIE.

DENNISTOUN,
 *November, 1907.*

# CONTENTS.

| CHAPTER | PAGE |
|---|---|
| I.—Boyhood Days, | 9 |
| II.—Paisley Clubs and Characters, | 27 |
| III.—Glasgow in the "Thirties," | 39 |
| IV.—Old Glasgow Characters, | 47 |
| V.—The Bread Riots, | 62 |
| VI.—The First Royal Visit to Glasgow, | 74 |
| VII.—Some Glasgow Clubs, | 87 |
| VIII.—Photographing Notabilities, | 101 |
| IX.—Advances in Photography, | 114 |
| X.—Recollections of Dr. Livingstone, | 130 |
| XI.—My Photographic Inventions, | 145 |

# LIST OF ILLUSTRATIONS.

| | PAGE |
|---|---|
| John Urie, | *Frontispiece* |
| Handloom Weaver and Draw-boy, | *facing* 13 |
| The Paisley Encyclopædia Club, | ,, 27 |
| "Hawkie" at the Briggate Well, | ,, 48 |
| The Bread Riots, 1848, | ,, 68 |
| John Robertson, Maker of the Engine for the "Comet," | ,, 106 |

# Reminiscences of 80 Years.

## CHAPTER I.

**BOYHOOD DAYS.**

MY recollection of events goes back over a period of more than eighty years. The reign of George III. was just drawing to its close when I first saw the light of day in Paisley, in the year 1820. And what a host of memories crowd upon me as I look back across the years that are gone into the void, memories that are pleasant and sad by turn. I think of the stirring movements and vast social progress that I have been privileged to watch in their growth and fulfilment. Across the years it seems difficult sometimes to realise how wide is the gulf which bridges the early nineteenth and the early twentieth centuries.

Ours was a Covenanting stock, and my great-grandfather was one of the number who laid down their lives for the cause. He was a printer in Glasgow, and editor of the first newspaper published in the city. His sad fate was to be shot at Polmadie for his adherence to the principles of the Covenant, and, along with three others who suffered martyrdom at the time, he was buried in Cathcart churchyard, where a large tablet still commemorates the event.

My father was a handloom weaver in Paisley, of the same stern and upright race as the men who fought at Bothwell Brig and Aird's Moss, and many a time did I hear from his lips the story of the struggle for religious liberty which agitated Scotland in the killing times.

He was one of those capitalists on a modern scale who were then known as " sma' corks." He had a modest cottage in Wellmeadow Street, opposite what was known as Urie's pump well. I can remember the wives of that part of the town assembling in knots at certain hours of the day to get the domestic supply of water and to exchange greetings and gossip. My father's cottage consisted of a but and a ben. On the one side of the passage was the kitchen and living-room, while on the other was the weaving-shop. The bedrooms were in the attics above. In the weaving-shop there stood six looms. The usual custom of "sma' corks" then was not to employ men to work the looms, but to let them out and charge so much for their use. As far as I remember, the rent which my father derived from each of the spare looms was the modest sum of a shilling a week. Industrial enterprise was of a much less complex character in those days, and the fine art of sub-contracting was almost unknown. The looms were pretty old, for they had been set up and worked by my grandfather. In the living-rooms almost every inch of space was covered with pictures of sacred subjects.

Of schooling I had little. For about six weeks I attended Wee Willie Aitken's school in Castle Street, where I was initiated into the three R's, with a few hints regarding other subjects, such as drawing painting, and astronomy. Wee Willie, who was a clever little man and a very good teacher, was rather fond of astronomy, and the ceiling of the school was painted over with representations of the sun, moon, and stars; and he used to give us lessons on the solar system, indicating with his pointer the relative positions of the heavenly bodies. So far as reading was concerned, the Bible was our only text-book, but we had a regular spelling-book. We were taught to make our own pens, for we still depended on the gray goose for our writing implements. Our great object was to make the pen with the fewest possible cuts of the knife. Five cuts were considered all that were necessary to transform a quill into a pen. Willie taught all the scholars himself. There were about a hundred on an average, of all ages and all stages of advancement, but none were neglected. The backward boys and those who were exceptionally bright received most attention, the mediocre crowd being allowed to jog along together. For our instruction we paid fees at the rate of threepence a week, or three shillings a quarter. That was the average rate, but some paid as little as a penny a week.

Willie Aitken afterwards opened an infant school in the town, and turned over the management of his other seminary to his brother-in-law. This venture was not a success, and he soon after began business as a bookseller in High Street opposite Storie Street. But he found bookselling even more precarious than teaching infants, and after some time that business had also to be given up.

My schooldays over, I started to work as a drawboy in my father's weaving-shop. After a few weeks

Handloom Weaver and Draw-boy.

# The Resurrectionist Scare.

at this job, my father set me to work a loom. At that time he was doing a good deal of work for a silk manufacturer named Fulton. I was put to making shawl fringes. But in a short time I rebelled against weaving altogether. The work was too monotonous, and I determined that I would be something better than a weaver. But before dealing with my beginnings in business, let me recall some stirring events of my boyhood.

The most exciting experiences of my boyhood days were in connection with the resurrectionist scare and cholera riots. I was but a young callant then, and three-quarters of a century has elapsed since I helped to smash the windows of the doctors'. houses in Paisley, but these events are deeply graven in my memory, and I can recall them as though they happened but yesterday.

It is quite impossible for people in these days to realise the horror and indignation caused by the diabolical outrages of the grave robbers. In the cities they stirred the people to fury, and even in quiet country districts the ghoulish deeds of the night prowlers roused the passions of all as nothing else could have done.

The revelations at the trial of Burke and Hare caused a profound sensation throughout the country.

A feeling of alarm and uneasiness was created, which spread, as reports began to be circulated, about graves being robbed and bodies being carried away for dissection. As a laddie, I used to hear the weavers in my father's shop talk with indignation of the doctors who encouraged this diabolical traffic in human remains.

Many and many a time in the long forenights of winter, after the day's work was done, did I sit by the fire listening to the stories told by my father and his visitors of the doings of the resurrectionists. This topic, with the Reform Bill and the prevailing depression in the weaving trade, monopolised conversation, and many were the speculations as to what would happen if the resurrectionists should try to rifle graves in Paisley.

At last the dreaded event actually happened. One dark winter day it was discovered that a grave had been opened by resurrectionists in a churchyard in Oakshaw Street, and the body of a young woman named Helen Duncan, which had been buried only four days previously, had been taken away.

The miscreants had evidently been afraid of detection, and had left the graveyard hurriedly after securing the corpse, for the grave was only half-filled up, and the grave clothes had not even

## A Ghastly Discovery.

been hidden away. They lay about in disorder as they had been torn from the corpse. I may state that as the law then stood the stealing of a body was not a punishable offence, but the theft of grave clothes was.

As soon as the news spread I made my way with other laddies of the town to the graveyard, impelled by curiosity to view the scene of these ghoulish operations. The town was in a ferment, and many of the looms stood idle that day, while the weavers went down to the graveyard in Oakshaw Street to discuss the turn of affairs.

As soon as he learned the terrible news, the father of the dead girl set out for Glasgow to try and recover the body of his daughter. He visited all the likely places, but without success, and returned at night weary and sick at heart.

When he had come home, a young man went and informed him that he had heard some very suspicious noises in a garret adjoining the one he occupied. He told how he had been awakened about three o'clock in the morning with a sound as of two men carrying a heavy burden upstairs. He listened, and heard them drag their burden along the floor of the garret into a corner. They exchanged a few words and then left. The garret was used as a lumber-room, and the door was not locked or secured in any way.

What a task was this for the bereaved father, thus wantonly bereft even of his dead! Getting the assistance of his brother, the father at once followed up this clue. One remained on guard outside the suspected house while the other went for the police.

Cautiously the little company crept upstairs, and one may imagine what the feelings of the unhappy father were as they proceeded upon their sad mission.

The door of the garret was opened by a policeman, and all passed inside. Nothing was to be seen but a heap of rubbish in a corner. One of the policemen went forward to make closer investigation, and found among the rubbish a sack. This was opened with apprehension, and with a gasp of horror the poor fellow recognised the pallid features of his daughter.

A great crowd waited at the foot of the stair when the body was brought down and conveyed to the Police Office. It seemed as if all Paisley were there that dark December night, and they surged up in the wake of the police as they carried the remains to the office.

It was a pity that no one thought of remaining

near the house, for scarcely half an hour elapsed after the departure of the police with the stolen body when two strangers heavily muffled in cloaks went up to the garret. Borrowing a candle from a woman in a neighbouring house, they proceeded upstairs.

One was overheard to say to the other, "It's off; let us begone." As they were going away, they steadfastly concealed their faces from observation, and as there were only a few women about they got off. The body of the young woman was re-interred and the matter carefully investigated, but the resurrectionists were never got.

The horror which this event caused in the breasts of young and old alike can scarcely be realised. I was then a laddie about nine years old, and as curious to see things and as fond of an adventure as most lads of that age, but I remember that winter not many of us cared to pass a graveyard after nightfall. If any business took us out late, we cast many sidelong glances at the stones in the graveyards as we hurried along, half-fearing, half-expecting to see the grim figure of a resurrectionist among the tombs.

But the older members of the community soon took active steps to prevent another such occurrence.

Meetings were held in the town, and it was agreed to form clubs for the protection of the dead. The proposal was entered into with vigour, and such was the fear inspired by the resurrectionists that within a year these clubs had no fewer than seven thousand members. Each member paid sixpence on joining and a penny per quarter thereafter. With the money thus collected, big wooden boxes were got as guardhouses for each graveyard. These boxes were very comfortable, and were fitted with grates for fires when necessary. The members of the clubs took their turn of watching the graveyards.

My father was a member of one of these clubs, and, of course, took his turn with the rest at watching. The fear which the doings of the resurrectionists had inspired gradually subsided, and I remember on several occasions pleading with my father to be allowed to go with him when it was his night on the watch. These entreaties, however, always met with a stern refusal, and the order to get off to bed at once.

These midnight vigils were not, if report was true, so monotonous and distasteful as might have been thought. Many stories of high jinks came out. The watch were generally provided with a bottle of whisky and a blunderbuss to ward off fancied and actual dangers. The young blades of the town soon began to take advantage of the loneliness of the mort guard and the nerve-shattering nature of their business to play all sorts of pranks on them.

They appeared among the tombs in white sheets; they let out blood-curdling yells or ghostly wailing with the intention of frightening the guard. Sometimes the ruse was successful, but more often the discharge of the blunderbuss in the direction of the would-be ghost sent the practical jokers scurrying off to their homes.

The clubs did their work admirably, and no case of body-snatching occurred in the town. In other places the same success did not follow. I remember hearing of a clever ruse practised on the guard. One night a woman came up to the graveyard, and, with much weeping and wailing, prepared to hang herself from the railings. The guard interfered, and tried to persuade the woman to go home, but all to no purpose. She persisted in declaring that she was going to hang herself. The watchmen, to prevent a tragedy, took the woman to her home, spending a considerable amount of time in this humanitarian duty. On returning to their post, however, they were horrified to find that during their absence the graveyard had been entered and a body taken away.

The watching of the graveyards continued for several years. In the spring of 1831, the churchyard of Renfrew was entered and the body of a woman stolen. This caused a great sensation in Paisley, and it was freely rumoured that the body of a young lad who had been drowned had been made away with by the resurrectionists. The grave was opened, but it was found intact, and the Paisley watchers took credit to themselves that body-snatching could not be practised when they were on guard.

I may say here that the clubs for the protection of the dead existed in Paisley till 1836, when they were finally dissolved; and it was agreed to allow the watchmen's boxes to remain in the graveyards for the convenience of any who might be disposed to keep watch over the graves of their friends.

It was in 1832 that the cholera plague, which had been travelling over Europe, reached Paisley, and caused considerable terror among the populace. I have reason to remember it well, for it is associated with an exciting episode in my career. We had ample warning of the coming of the plague, for it had spread over a considerable part of England before it came as far north as Paisley.

There was then little or no attention paid to sanitation, but no sooner did the plague make its appearance in a district than active measures were at once taken to cleanse the filthy back premises of our towns and villages. It was in February, 1832, that it broke out in Paisley, and, within four days of the first case being detected, there were eighteen cases and nine deaths. Then, for several months, there were on an average about thirty fresh cases weekly, and a proportionate number of deaths.

Among the remedial measures taken was one which had a sort of weird fascination for me at the time. The Magistrates decided to fumigate the town with diluted sulphuric acid and chloride of lime. No time was lost in carrying out this plan. Six large tubs filled with the mixture were placed on barrows, and, preceded by torches, these were wheeled through the streets and lanes of the town. The thoroughfares were not so broad as they are now, and the spectacle of these strange processions of torch-bearers and fumigators lingers in my memory. Many of the householders opened their windows to admit the pungent fumes of the sulphuric acid to their houses.

In spite of these precautions, the people died fast, and, as is usually the case, the poor died faster than those who were well-to-do. The Magistrates found it necessary to issue a proclamation that the common ground in the city graveyards would be closed, and that for those who could not afford private lairs, a part of the town land in the Moss on the Greenock Road was set apart. We boys used to go down and play about the Moss, but when it became a cemetery for the plague victims, we were well warned by our parents not to go there. We did not always heed their warnings, however, and sometimes viewed, from what we considered a safe distance, the interment of the victims of the plague.

I remember well that Sunday morning in March when the discovery was made that the graves in the Moss were being tampered with. Some men had been strolling about the part allotted to the cholera victims when they discovered two shovels, together with a small piece of cord, having an iron hook attached to it. This was considered clear proof that the resurrectionists had been at work, for how else could their presence there be explained?

The town was soon in a ferment. The implements were brought up to the Cross, and the manner in which they had been found was described to a

## The Cholera Riots.

gathering crowd. During that day the Moss was visited by large numbers of the weavers of the town. I may say that among a large section of the community the medical profession was then looked upon with profound distrust. The fact that some members of the profession at any rate were in the habit of buying, for dissection, bodies stolen from graveyards, caused them to be regarded with abhorrence.

In Paisley the suspicion was freely expressed, absurd though it was, that the doctors were responsible for the deaths of many of the cholera patients, and when the discovery on the Moss was made, it seemed to justify these suspicions.

At an early hour next morning, a large crowd assembled in the Moss, determined to find out whether the graves had been violated or not. The first grave opened contained an empty coffin. The implements found on the previous day were exhibited in a shop window, and caused great excitement, which was increased tenfold when the result of the operations on the Moss became known. I was early abroad that morning, and found the streets filled with excited weavers, whose execrations of the doctors were loud and deep. As with one accord, we set off for the Moss to see for ourselves what the truth of the matter was.

The men at the burial-ground showed us the empty coffin, which had an extraordinary effect upon the crowd. In a large gathering like that, and in the condition that they were, exaggerated reports flew from mouth to mouth. It was stated that seven or eight coffins had been found empty. Then a man got up and proposed that they march back into the town, take the empty coffin with them, and demand vengeance on those who had been responsible for this outrage.

A deep roar of approval greeted this proposal. The men had been accustomed to marching in procession, for they had not long ago in this way demonstrated their approval of the Reform Bill. But this procession was a wilder one than any I had ever taken part in. The empty coffin was carried shoulder high by those in front.

As we marched along the road back to the town, the fences were torn down, and the people armed themselves with stobs and bars, and searched the roads and fields on the route for suitable stones. Clearly there were all the elements here of a serious disorder.

As we came into the town, the Magistrates, fearing what the consequences might be, came out and tried to pacify the crowd. Some threw aside the stobs they were carrying, but the majority were in no mood to parley. The police were stoned, and forced to seek shelter in a house in St. James Street, the windows of which were smashed without the least hesitation. That was the beginning of the fray, which did not end until some four hundred panes of glass had been broken.

We marched through the narrow streets, sweeping all before us, and destroying as much of the property of the doctors as we could. Along with nearly all the other boys of the town, I marched along through streets, smashing glass without restraint, our love of mischief finding free course. The Cholera Hospital, in Oakshaw Street, was visited, and the cholera van seized, and dragged along in front of the procession. The van was ultimately broken up, and put into the River Cart.

By and by, however, our operations received a check. Word came that the military had arrived, and when we turned into the Square, we found a regiment of soldiers drawn up. For the first time in my life I heard the Riot Act read. There was, however, no need to follow it with a volley of ball cartridge. The weavers had taken the vengeance they desired, and they dispersed quietly to their homes. By four o'clock in the afternoon, the town was quiet again.

Thus ended what was one of the most exciting days in my life, and one of the most thrilling episodes in the history of Paisley in my time.

THE PAISLEY ENCYCLOPÆDIA CLUB.

## CHAPTER II.

### PAISLEY CLUBS AND CHARACTERS.

ROUND the old town of Paisley many of my fondest memories cling. In its social aspects, there was much that was quaint and interesting to be noted.

I have already dealt with the work of the Paisley Protection of the Dead Club. There were many other clubs in the old town in these days, whose origin and objects were not of a grim and tragic nature.

The want of circulating libraries was filled by numerous book clubs. Each member contributed one book to the common stock. The books were exchanged monthly at the club meeting-place, where discussions on their contents and current topics were indulged in.

I can well remember almost eighty years ago being the honoured guest at the meeting of the Encyclopædia Club, of which my father was an enthusiastic member. My father was dressing himself in his Sunday clothes one evening, and as I was his companion in most of his outings, I knew he must be going somewhere in particular.

"Where are you going, dad?" I asked.

"To the club," he answered quite snappishly.

"Well, I will go with you."

"No, you won't," was the reply.

I began to howl, knowing what the result would be. My mother here broke in—

"Let the laddie go with you to the club door."

"Very well," said my father. "Take that book," pointing to a volume of the *Encyclopædia Britannica*, "to Johnny Blair's, and say I will be in a little."

I took the big book in my arms—it seemed to me just like my grandfather's family Bible—and went to Johnny Blair's, where I laid it down on the counter, saying, "There's your book. Father will be here in a little."

"Take it into the big room," said the shopman.

I carried the book into the clubroom, where were seated round a long table a number of men in their Sunday clothes, with Wull Pattison, the blacksmith, sitting at the head. Wull and I were old friends, and when I went to the smithy with a sheep's head to be singed, he always said, "Keep the penny an' buy a scone with it, Johnny."

I laid the book down on the table among a lot of others, when the smith got his eye on me, and said, "Come awa' up to the fire, Johnny, and warm your taes," and I sat supporting the chair all night.

I can remember the men kept up a continual stream of talk about the Reform Bill, Johnny Russell, Earl Grey, and other political leaders of the time.

By and by the wee barber got up, and, thumping on the table, cried out, "Landlord, anither gill and a bottle o' sma'."

The gill and the sma' are brought in, with a biscuit. The barber, laying down sixpence, got a penny back.

"Gi'e the laddie the biscuit," says the schoolmaster. "And the penny," adds the blacksmith.

They then went on talking about James Watt and the steam engine, the Jacquard loom, and the spinning jenny, till I fell fast asleep, but was aye roused up now and then with the thumping on the table and "anither gill and a bottle o' sma'."

That night I went home with my pockets full of biscuits and a gowpenful of pennies, and from that day to this I have been an enthusiastic clubman.

Other clubs flourished in Paisley in those days, and through them I got to know a number of literary and artistic notabilities. One of the best known of these was called the "Literary and Convivial Association." To tell the truth, there was not much conviviality as we understand the word now. The members were rather an abstemious lot. They never met in a public house, but provided their own refreshments. Not more than one glass was allowed each member between eight and ten o'clock, and those arriving after nine o'clock got no refreshment. The outstanding man in this club was William Motherwell, the poet, the author of "Jeanie Morrison":—

> " O, dear, dear Jeanie Morrison,
>     The thochts o' bygane years
> Shall fling their shadows ower my path,
>     And blind my e'e wi' tears;
> They blind my e'e wi' saut, saut tears,
>     And sair and sick I pine
> As memory idly summons up
>     The blithe blinks o' langsyne.

> " I wonder, Jeanie, often yet,
>     When sitting on that bink,
> Cheek touchin' cheek, loof lock'd in loof,
>     What our wee heads could think
> When baith bent doon ower ae braid page,
>     Wi' ae buik on our knee;
> Thy lips were on thy lesson, but
>     My lesson was in thee."

The Jeanie Morrison that Motherwell immortalised in this tender poem was his sweetheart when a boy at school in Edinburgh. When I was a lad, Motherwell was Sheriff Clerk-Depute of Renfrewshire and editor of the *Paisley Advertiser*. He was a grand hand at telling a story, especially about ghosts, in which he had a firm belief. He went to Glasgow in 1830 to be editor of the *Courier*.

Among other members of this club were James Yool, editor of the *Gaberlunzie*; John Fraser, editor of the *Renfrewshire Chronicle*; John Nelson, the book printer; and Dr. Thomas Lyle, the author of that pretty song, "Let us haste to Kelvingrove, Bonnie Lassie, O."

Noel Paton, afterwards the famous painter, I remember meeting in Paisley. He was a fine, strapping young fellow then, quiet, and diligent with his pencil. He was working as a designer in Brown & Sharp's warehouse, and was an enthusiastic member of the Paisley Burns Club, which met in the Sun Tavern. This was one of the earliest of the Burns Clubs in this country. Among its founders were Tannahill, the poet; R. A. Smith, the famous musician, who set Tannahill's charming songs to music; and Alexander Borland, who accompanied the unfortunate poet from Glasgow to Paisley on the night of his death.

At the Burns Club meetings Noel Paton was for ever making sketches. It was when in Paisley that he did the illustrations for A. Park's poem of "Silent Love," which first established his fame as an artist. One of the stanzas of a poem that he wrote in after-life comes to my memory—

> "I see the infinite loveliness
>   Of God's fair universe—can bless
>   His creatures in their blessedness
>     Despite my own heart's aching;
>   But never more my soul may know,
>   The thrill of sympathy, the glow
>   Of love that stirred it long ago,
>     In youth's divine upwaking."

These and many other notable men rise up in my recollection as I think of those early days. There was a man we knew in Paisley as "Cutler Jock, the Quaker." His name was John Henderson, and he had some literary powers, acting as correspondent to the *Reformer's Gazette*, which was then edited by Peter Mackenzie. He kept a well-stocked shop of cutlery, and sharpened almost all the butcher's knives in the old town. Jock was a strenuous advocate of the deepening of the Cart, so as to make Paisley a seaport town.

## Caldwell, the Printer.

The wife of Geordie Caldwell, a printer in Paisley, was also a bit of a character. She kept the Teetotal Tower, a building between Paisley and Renfrew. There she served out lemonade and ginger beer to the young lads who frequented her place. I remember her well as she dispensed her hospitality attired in a silk dress, with the heads of stockings drawn up over her arms as sleeves.

The attractions of the place were greatly enhanced by a camera obscura, to which admission was gained on payment of a penny. You got a fine view of the surrounding country in that darkened room.

George Caldwell's children were sent out to school or to play chained to each other, so that the one could not run away from the other.

Among the characters of Paisley I must not forget to mention Wee Willie Fulton, the proprietor of Glenfield. Willie was a homely body, but a shrewd and keen business man, and though he rose from being a humble weaver to be the owner of a large estate and the head of a prosperous business he never forgot the old Scottish dialect nor the friends of his youth. He knew Tannahill well, and used to declare that he was the prettiest shuttler he had ever seen. There was an evenness in the way he pitched the shot from which he never varied, and he had a wee box on the top of his loom in which he kept his writings, and he had a slate which hung on his loompost, and on which he used to jot down his thoughts.

"I hae seen Robin Tannahill," Willie once declared to my old friend Kelso Hunter, the cobbler-artist, "sittin' suppin' his parritch aff his knee oot o' a bowl soomin' wi' milk. I think that nae ither meal has the grandeur o' parritch, an' nae table so sensible as the knees, haudin' steady wi' one han' an' suppin' wi' the ither, an' the medium o' conveyance a horn spoon."

The stirring events that marked the passing of the great Reform Bill of 1831 come vividly to my recollection. Like most other weaving communities, Paisley was an intensely Radical town, and the sympathies of the weavers were all with the Reformers. Processions and demonstrations in favour of the Bill were held everywhere, and Paisley was not behindhand in this respect.

It was a great event in Paisley when several thousands of weavers marched to Glasgow to join in a huge demonstration in favour of the Reform Bill, which took place at the Green. I was present with my father on that occasion. The stir and the excitement, the flying of banners and the blaring of bugles, made a lasting impression on me. One man in Paisley made a small fortune that day. He was Geordie Caldwell, whose principal business was in printing ballads and broadsheets, with sketches, for sale on the streets. All the demonstrators were wearing broad red sashes with the word "Reform" printed in big letters along the sash. Geordie made a specialty of printing these badges, and he and his old wooden press were kept hard at it impressing "Reforms" at a cost to the reformers of twopence a sash.

The first election in Paisley after the passing of the Reform Bill was a great event. Sir John Maxwell of Pollock stood as the Liberal candidate, and was opposed by a Mr. M'Kerrel, who represented the Tory side. I was not deeply interested in politics then, but one feature of the election had a great attraction for us boys. There was then no Corrupt Practices Act, and it was quite a common thing for a candidate and his agent to go along the street flinging coppers and silver broadcast among the children.

I remember Sir John and his committee going down Wellmeadow Street canvassing for voters. They were scattering handfuls of coins, and you may be sure that we followed their proceedings very closely. In the scramble I managed to secure half-a-crown, which represented to me untold wealth. For days after I was living a life of luxury, much to the advantage of the retailers of candy.

Among other more tragic incidents of my boyhood days, I can recall the execution of Craig and Brown for breaking into Foxbar House near Renfrew. The poor fellows were hanged in front of the County Buildings, a place then commonly known as Jail Square. As usual on such occasions, there was a large turn out of the inhabitants.

Steam navigation was in its infancy, but Paisley was provided even then with a passenger steamer. This vessel was named the *Cupid*, and nicknamed *Stupid* on account of its propensity for running into sandbanks. It went down the Cart and then down the Clyde as far as Rothesay. We boys used to get on board the boat as she was leaving the harbour at the Sneddon and sail down as far as Inchinnan Bridge. The river, which is very narrow at this point, was crossed by a swing-bridge. So close did the vessel run to the bridge, that we had no difficulty in stepping off at this point, and then we made for home. The *Cupid* took almost twelve hours to sail to Rothesay and back.

# First Railway Journey.

I shall never forget my first railway journey. All the railways in and around Glasgow were made within my recollection, but when I first came to the city I travelled by the canal boat. The Garnkirk railway, however, was constructed when I was a fair-sized lad, and I greatly desired to have a ride on this new and wonderful conveyance. Several other boys and I had been gathering up our pennies for some time in order to get this treat, and when we heard that the British fleet was lying off Leith we thought we would go there. Accordingly we went by canal-boat to Glasgow, and going out to St. Rollox we bought tickets for Coatbridge.

It seemed a long, rough journey, for the carriages were just like cattle trucks. We had to stand all the way, and got jostled till our bones were sore. On arriving at Coatbridge we left the train and tramped to Bathgate. Here we refreshed ourselves with a large basinful of brose. We went right on to Leith, and wanted to get on board one of the vessels of the fleet, but found that the ferryman wanted a bigger fee to take us than our finances could afford. We accordingly turned sorrowfully back and walked to Paisley, where our friends were anxiously waiting our return.

I remember as a lad seeing the men blasting the tunnels at Bishopton, on the Glasgow and Greenock Railway, and I also have recollections of seeing the collapse of a newly-constructed bridge in Paisley, on the same line. The arch had not been properly keyed, and it fell down with an awful smash as soon as the supports were taken out.

## CHAPTER III.

### GLASGOW IN THE "THIRTIES."

GLASGOW was the city of my dreams. Lying so close to our doors, it exercised a great fascination over me. Many a time I had been in it on a visit, and I delighted to walk through its busy streets, and to take note of its quaint places and queer characters. Often did I long for the day when I should be able to live and work within its bounds.

At last the long wished opportunity came. A cousin of ours, who frequently visited my father, had a tavern in the Briggate. Knowing that I was greatly dissatisfied in the prospect of being a weaver, and that I was anxious to get a job in Glasgow, he urged my father to allow him to take me into his tavern as assistant. It was not the kind of work my father wished to see me at, but the solicitations of my cousin, backed up by my own pleadings, overcame his scruples, and he at last gave his consent.

I was greatly delighted at the prospect. My father stipulated that my cousin should send me to the night school to make up for the want of the instruction that he and my mother were giving me to supplement my meagre schooling. I was to live with my cousin in his country-house in Crown Street, and go home for the week-ends.

Very proud was I when the preparations for my departure were commenced. The whip the cat tailor was brought into the house to make me a stylish blue suit, for I was to have a brand new rig-out. When the hour for departure came, I was handed into the canal boat by my anxious relatives and sorrowing companions, who envied me my good luck.

I was now entirely in my element selling drams to the queer customers that frequented the classic thoroughfare of the Briggate. Near the Gilderoy Court was Mr. Marshall's famous eating-house, while opposite was the Goosedubs, the birthplace of Graham Gilbert, the artist. Nearby was the Briggate pump, at which might be daily seen a strange figure supported on a stilt and a staff.

This was "Hawkie," the greatest wit I ever met in the streets of Glasgow. Many a dram I sold him in those days, and many another I slipped to him unobserved, putting a glass of water into the barrel so that my master should not be the loser by my generosity.

My reign at the Briggate Tavern was brief. I had been dispensing spirits for three months, when being home for Sunday I had some words with my brother Bob. In the heat of our quarrel I was airing some expressions never before heard in our house which I had picked up in the Briggate, when my father turned on me, and said—" You must come to the kirk with me. You are getting rather smart; you will have to leave that place and come home to Paisley." It was a blow to me, but I had no option but submit.

Soon after I came home, I started my apprenticeship as a stereotyper with Mr. Neilson, a printer in Paisley. In those days we stereotyped by pouring liquid stucco over the face of the type, and allowing it to harden. Then we took this stucco mould off and poured the melted metal over it. When the new system of stereotyping with paper machie moulds was introduced, Neilson was one of the first to take it up, and I believe I was the first stereotyper in Scotland to practice the new method.

My apprenticeship was to last for seven years, but I did not serve it out. The first year I enjoyed the modest salary of two shillings and sixpence a week. The second year it was three shillings, and it was to creep up by sixpence a week every year during the term of my apprenticeship. But after three or four years' service I was in practical charge of the stereotyping department, the journeymen having all left one after another. I was then receiving four shillings a week, but on my representing that I was underpaid for having the responsibility of this department on my shoulders, Mr. Neilson raised my wages at a bound to what I then considered the princely salary of twelve shillings a week. After three months of this, Mr. Neilson received a big order from Francis Orr & Sons. Mr. Neilson intimated that he would have to get in a journeyman from Glasgow, and that I would have to go back to my old wages. This arrangement did not suit my views, and accordingly I left.

At this time all the wooden blocks for illustrations had to be brought from London, there being no wood engraver in the West of Scotland. I felt that I could turn out as good work as we got from the Metropolis, and accordingly, having read up all I could about the process, I resolved to try.

For a start I began making the big wooden types which are used in printing bills and posters. These

# My First Commission.

I made and sold to the printers in Glasgow. Then I came back to the city again, and set up business in a shop in the Gallowgate, in the building now occupied by the Army Recruiting Office. My place of business was then close to my living room.

My first commission was in connection with one of the most exciting incidents in the annals of Glasgow. The city had been greatly disturbed by the Bishopbriggs murder, when the foreman of a squad of navvies engaged in making the Edinburgh and Glasgow railway was brutally murdered by several of his men. Two of those implicated, Dennis Doolan and Patrick Redding, were sentenced to death for their share of the crime. On the day before the murderers were to be executed, Mr. Brookman, who had been foreman in the well-known printing works of Foulis & Co., but who then carried on business for himself at the corner of Union Street and Argyle Street, came to me and said—

"Could you not make an engraving of the execution that is coming on?"

"I will try," I said, and it was agreed that we should go out to take a sketch of the scaffold early in the morning.

We went accordingly, and I took a sketch of the gibbet. Then I engraved the picture, sketching in the victims from memory, and it was printed on a broadsheet along with "The last dying speech and confession of Dennis Doolan." Newspapers were scarce and dear, for the stamp duty and paper duty still remained, so that our broadside, which was put out at the popular price of a penny, sold by the thousand on the day of execution. The speech and confession attributed to Dennis were purely imaginary.

The execution was one of the most impressive sights of its kind that ever were witnessed in Glasgow.

The condemned men were confined in the South Prison, as the Justiciary Buildings, Jail Square, were then called. By five o'clock on that May morning the crowd had begun to gather in front of that gloomy building. The usual order was that an execution should take place between the hours of eight and ten o'clock in the morning, but owing to the distance that had to be travelled before the place of execution could be reached, the order was altered from eight o'clock to two. The gallows, which had been taken out from Glasgow Prison, had been put up, so that the men should die looking down on the spot where they had killed the unfortunate ganger.

There were thousands in the Saltmarket and the High Street by seven o'clock, when Sheriff Alison, accompanied by a troop of cavalry and two companies of infantry, rode down to the prison, and by eight o'clock, when the procession was formed, the streets along which it would pass was one continuous flood of humanity. The pavements were crowded, and at every window and on every housetop was to be seen the same array of eager, anxious faces.

Then the procession started. First came a body of cavalry, then the Sheriff, Lord Provost, and Magistrates, then the executioner, then the condemned men, in their cart with their coffins beside them, and accompanied by their spiritual advisers, and, last of all, the city marshals.

The cart on which the condemned men sat pinioned loosely was guarded on all sides by strong detachments of cavalry, infantry, and police, the infantry having their bayonets fixed. One would have thought that some important military operation was to have been performed, for the small army consisted of 1200 infantry, 600 cavalry, and two guns. It was clear that the Government were determined that any attempt at rescue would be frustrated.

It was certainly a weird procession. The white faces of the condemned men in the cart drew the gaze of all as they sat, chained together hand and foot, with downcast heads. Over the tramp, tramp of horses and men, those nearest to the cart could hear the priests intoning as they read aloud to the wretched prisoners.

The execution took place about half-past nine o'clock. Redding died without a struggle, but Doolan's agonies were painful to witness. After hanging for forty minutes, the bodies were cut down and placed in their coffins. The mournful procession was then re-formed, and returned to the city as it had come.

# CHAPTER IV.

### OLD GLASGOW CHARACTERS.

THE streets of Glasgow are in many respects less interesting to-day than they were when I first knew them. There is more noise and stir and bustle—evidence of a greater earnestness in the pursuit of gain. But with all this feverish rush after wealth, we have lost some of those features which made the streets so dear to me in the days of my boyhood. Year by year our thoroughfares become more modern and more respectable, and the people one meets in them more business-like and more commonplace.

We have no characters now. They are all gone, those worthies that made our streets so picturesque, and proved to me a never-failing source of interest. "Hawkie," with his ready tongue and his unquenchable thirst; "Old Malabar," with his Oriental robe and cup and ball; "Rab Ha," the famous glutton; Jamie Blue, Wee Jamie Wallace, "The Teapot," and many others, have disappeared for ever, and with them the race of characters may be said to have died out.

The prince of gangrels was "Old Hawkie." No one was in a better position to meet this worthy than those who were engaged in the sale of drink —for "Hawkie" dearly loved whisky, and made no secret of the fact. His clothes were dirty and ragged, his battered hat was worn well down on his nose, his face was unshaven and showed no intimate acquaintance with water. But despite his unkempt and almost uncouth appearance, he seldom wanted an audience. In a combat of wits he always emerged victorious. His sayings formed one of the commonest subjects of conversation in the city, and it may be said that no one was better known or more frequently quoted in his day than this poor shrivelled mendicant. He and I were, for a time, on friendly terms, and I was not long in learning his history.

His real name was William Cameron, and he was born in the parish of St. Ninians, in Stirling. As he early showed remarkable cleverness, his parents gave him an excellent education, being the more desirous of giving him a good start in life because he had been permanently crippled by a fall when an infant. He was apprenticed to a tailor, but he did

"Hawkie" at the Briggate Well.

Page 48.

not care for the work, and his master had no great opinion of his abilities.

As he used to say—" My maister hinted that it wasna likely that I wad ever mak' saut to my kail southerin' claith thegither, and if the shears were run through every stitch o' my indentures it wadna brak his hert. Thinks I tae masel', there's a pair o' us, as the coo said to the cuddy, an' my crutch will do the job as well as your clippers, so I laid the whup to ma stilt and took the road hame."

For a while before he became a speech-seller, he essayed various jobs—teaching miners' bairns, starring Fife with a company of strolling actors, mending and selling crockery. Each was tried in turn, but none was followed for long. Then he gravitated to Glasgow and took up the business of selling cheap literature in the streets.

Before the advent of the penny newspaper these chapbooks and leaflets were very popular. "Hawkie" had considerable gifts as an elocutionist, having a fine clear voice and almost perfect articulation. This, with his witty descriptions of the contents of his pamphlets, made him the most successful speech-crier in Glasgow. If a public execution were to take place, "Hawkie" was sure to be on the streets loaded with a huge bundle of the " Speech and Last

Dying Confession" of the unhappy felon. These he quickly disposed of at a halfpenny each.

But executions did not occur every day, and, failing such a stirring event, "Hawkie" retailed broadsheets of all kinds, some with crude and often coarse tales, some with political or personal lampoons in verse, some with old legends or stories. The titles of a few that "Hawkie" used to sell will give an idea of their contents. "Watty and Meg—A Cure for Ill Wives," "Janet Clinker's Oration on the wit of the Old Wives and the Pride of the Young Women," "The Trial and Burning of Maggie Lang, the Cardonald Witch," etc.

The nickname "Hawkie" was bestowed on him in Glasgow. Shortly after Cameron came to the city, a man named Ross created some sensation by predicting the destruction of the world in general and Glasgow in particular. Cameron worked up a scathing satire on the prophecies of this quack. He also went into the prophetic business, making his seer " Hawkie, a twa-year-auld quey frae Aberdour, in the county o' Fife."

This prophecy of "Hawkie" foretold the destruction of the Briggate by a flood of whisky. The flood would be so great, the prophet went on to state, that it would rise to the top flats of the highest houses in the street and drown the inhabitants. Many would attempt to escape in washing tubs, but, though numbers would be saved in that way, many of the women would be drowned by leaning over the sides of tubs and upsetting them in their eagerness to drink the whisky.

These prophecies proved a splendid speculation, and so much were the sayings of the gifted cow discussed that Willie was nicknamed "Hawkie," a sobriquet which he liked in preference to his own name.

In this connection I may say that, while I never saw whisky flooding the Briggate, I have waded in the waters of the Clyde, which overflowed and came up as far as that thoroughfare.

I can well remember "Hawkie" selling his cure for ill wives. "Without the least respect of persons," he would say, "I am here with the cure, and it costs only a bawbee. I needna waste my time describin' an ill wife to ye further than to state my simple opinion that an ill wife is the greatest evil that ony puir man can be cursed wi'. So I wad advise ony o' you wha are under the curse to come to me for the cure. Ony o' ye wha hae the curse o' an ill wife, an' are in want o' the bawbee to the bargain, step forrit and state your cases. Never let your modesty hurt your interest. Lay fause delicacy aside; be honest to yourselves, and get the curse removed."

At this appeal the halfpence would flow as the men laughingly held out their hands for "Hawkie's" little pamphlet. Then a half-intoxicated man would rate him. "You are an immoral character, sir, and a bad example to the youth, curse, cursing about wives the way you are doing."

"Hawkie" would take stock of his man for a minute, and then remark—"Frien', wis ye wantin' the cure? I see the mark of the beast on your forehead; but a guid wife wad be lost on the like o' you. Awa' hame and tak' a sleep afore ye gang to the kirk the morn."

"Hawkie's" description of the beggar's burial and dredgy (the funeral feast) was a masterpiece of its kind. He had a fine flow of picturesque, pithy language, as this part of the famous oration will show:—

"Next the hale clamjamfry of vagrants—for they're a' but beggars' bairns the best o' them—randies, thieves, big beggars, wee beggars, bane-gatherers and bowley-powleys, criers o' hanging speeches, wha generally should have been the subject o' their ain story, some wi' weans but a' wi' wallets; broken backs, hauf airms and nae airms, some wi' only hauf an e'e, some wi' mair e'en than Nature gi'ed them, and that is an e'e efter everything they can mak' their ain; snub noses, slit noses, and hauf noses, Roman noses, lang noses, some o' them like a chuckie stane, ithers like a jarganell pear, hawk noses and goose noses; an' mind ye, I dinna find fault wi' the last kind, for Nature does naething in vain, and put it there to suit the head; but whatever the size and description o' the neb, they could a' tak' their pick, for the hail concern, man and mither's son, had mouths, and when teeth were wantin' the deficit was mair than made up by desperate willin' gums."

"Hawkie" thus described the progress of a young man in crime after he has had his first experience of prison. "That is what I wad name the first step o' 'case-hardenin'.' Tammy meets with kindred souls there, and confinement is stripped o' its terrors. He comes out bolder and braver, and is on his arrival hame caress'd by his mither. Aweel, Tammy grows in everything but grace, and as his pith increases it is merely employed to remove movable property, and ere lang he spends the proceeds on his ain appetites—for sweetmeats and a turn in the Waterloo fly. Tammy has been sae aft before the Magistrates that 'habit and repute' is attached to his name instead o' 'esquire.' He is gettin' bigger, and a higher Court is recommended to inquire into his misdemeanours.

"But for a sicht o' the Lords. They hae arrived in the toun; great is the pomp and mockery. Guarded wi' sojers and policemen, the same as if they were vagabonds, wi' a band o' music playing the Rogues' March and a creature in front wi' a trumpet, toot, tootin' awa' to represent the day of judgment to fricht Tammy and the rest o' the puir wichts who are supposed to be lyin' tremblin' in the jail; and then the Judge himsel', as if he wasna ridiculous enough already, is buskit up like a scarecrow, wi' a wheen dyed cloots rowed aboot him an' a pickle sheep's woo' on the heid o' him, an' the advocates rowed up in black cloots as stiff like as mummies, an' a pickle woo on their heads tae, makin' them look like snawba's on the tap o' soot bags. It's a startlin' sort o' mental depravity in high places tryin' tae scaur actual depravity in the lower stratum o' life."

The Rev. Peter Henderson, who was at one time a minister in Pollokshaws, was on intimate terms with "Hawkie." They met in the poorhouse, where Mr. Henderson was in the habit of visiting before he was licensed to preach. After being licensed he was to start on a travelling mission to some out-of-the-way district which would take him away for six months. He paid a visit to the poorhouse to give the matron the news, and found "Hawkie" sitting by the fire, and reading to her from Allan Ramsay's "Gentle Shepherd."

The matron expressed regret that he was about to leave them, but pleasure at his advancement, adding, "But, dear me, you are a young man to be entrusted with such a sacred mission." Mr. Henderson was rather flattered by this remark, and, as "Hawkie" was surveying him very steadfastly, he expected that the mendicant shared these sentiments. But, lifting up his book, "Hawkie" observed, "Ou ay; he'll do weel enough. The creature will no be sax weeks at it till he be fleyin' the puir creatures wi' hell the same as if he had been born in't and brocht up in't a' his days."

This remark completely took the wind out of Mr. Henderson's sails, and he liked "Hawkie" ever after for thus reproving his vanity. Mr. Henderson, who had not met "Hawkie" for some time, stood up in the street once and gave him a penny, saying—

"I'm thinking, William, that you have forgotten me now."

"I'm no thinkin' that, Mr. Henderson," came the reply. "I make it a rule in my profession to know no man after the flesh. It's quite sufficient for my purpose that they ken me. But to let you ken that I hae na forgotten you, I may tell you that I am comin' oot to Pollokshaws some Sunday to preach a sermon in aid of the Sustentation Fund. I'm gaun to tak' my stand at your yett. I'll hae a white cloot aneath my auld hat that day. I hope you'll be liberal. I'll hae a' your flock as hearers on that occasion and yoursel' amang them, for nane o' them will leave me to follow you."

"Hawkie" died in the city poorhouse in September, 1851. A friend of mine saw him shortly before his death and gave me this account of his last meeting with the famous wit:—

"He was standing opposite the door of a whisky shop at the foot of the Saltmarket holding out his hand at his eyes' level. I had only one bawbee in the world, and it was in my pouch. His eye met mine, and instinctively I laid my last bawbee in 'Hawkie's' loof. He looked all round his audience, and in a plaintive tone of voice said, 'Cover that, some o' you.' There was no response. He looked in my face and said, 'Providence! An open hand, an open heart, an open door, a drouth, and the

# The Saltmarket.

means o' quenchin' it.' So saying, he crawled to the counter for a bawbee's worth of whisky."

Let me try to describe to you the Saltmarket as it existed in my early recollection. It was then a very important thoroughfare, and Bailie Nicol Jarvie's remark about its comforts could not then be quoted in irony as it is so often now. Many important business establishments stood there at that time. The warehouse kept by J. & W. Campbell, father and uncle of the present Prime Minister, was here. Wylie & Lochhead began their business in a small shop there, afterwards removing to Argyle Street. Near the head of the street was the Shakespeare Singing Saloon (most famous of the old free-and-easy places of entertainment, from which the modern music hall is evolved).

The Post Office was in Nelson Street, but a few years previously it had been located in Princes Street. It was a small concern before the days of penny postage and when the mails were largely carried by coach. Passing the Briggate, we came to Jail Square. At this time the slaughter-house was behind the jail, but previous to its erection cattle were killed in the street. When an ox was knocked down the butcher called out "Blood, blood, blood," so that the poor people who gathered about might catch the red fluid in their cans as it flowed from the slaughtered animal.

Here also was to be seen the gallows, a large wooden erection on wheels ready to be drawn to the front of the jail when Tam Young, the hangman, had a victim to operate on.

But the scene is changed. The great Glasgow Fair is about to begin. From all parts people come crowding to see the wonderful and varied exhibitions that line the Saltmarket during the great annual festival. There is no crowding of trains and steamboats for the coast or country, for Glasgow Fair is held in Glasgow, and Rothesay and Dunoon are not yet.

At the corner of the Saltmarket and Greendyke Streets stands Mumford's penny show, long one of the features of that quarter of the town. For many years after it ceased to be a "geggie," it remained one of the landmarks of the old Saltmarket, and was demolished only six years ago. During the Fair, special inducements are held out to visitors, part of the front boarding being lowered so as to form a platform, on which the orchestra performs. Old Dupaine, the proprietor, plays the bass fiddle in the interval between taking the coppers. You climb up a narrow stair at the corner in order to obtain admission.

"Just about to commence, ladies and gentlemen," the proprietor shouts a score of times while the house is filling. The actors and actresses parade the boards outside, dressed in all their finery, the funny man tickling the expectant crowd with jokes, and the "premiere danseuse" giving an occasional saltatory display. We pay our pennies, and on the invitation of the manager and chief actor we step inside to see the show.

One advantage of the old method of spending the Fair time is that you can get a great deal of entertainment for a small expenditure of cash. Popular prices rule at mostly all the shows. Near Mumford's geggie you may see Wombwell's wild beast caravans, and Ewing's Waxwork; beside them Cooke's Circus, while in other booths are jugglers and boxers, and those wonders of the age, Bosjesmen, natives of Africa, but more likely to be natives of our own islands than of the Dark Continent.

A friend and I once went in to see these so-called natives, and the showman inviting any gentleman who could speak the language to step forward and converse with them to show that there was no deception, my friend went up, and engaged in a burlesque confab with one of them, ending with, "Will you have a drink?" The South African native replied in excellent English, "I will go over to the club with you."

Other attractions of the Fair may be mentioned—the large theatre belonging to Anderson, the "Wizard of the North," the most noted juggler and illusionist that existed in those days, and D. P. Millar's Adelphi. Here some of the best actors and actresses on the stage were to be seen. Macready, the famous tragedian, and Miss Faucit, Mrs. Stirling, and many others of lesser note trod the boards of the old Adelphi.

It was here also that Miss Aitkin was brought out. She was the daughter of James Aitkin, then a teacher of elocution in Nelson Street. He was an actor of some note, and was famous for his acting of the part of "Wandering Steenie," in "The Rose of Ettrick Vale."

During the Fair there was to be seen from nearly every window in the Saltmarket, a notice to the effect that "penny reels" might be had within. This meant that for this humble sum a dance might be engaged in, and the householders in the main thoroughfare made a good deal of money by allowing the lads and lasses who paid their pennies to dance to the music of a wheezy concertina or a squeaky fiddle.

Around Jail Square were booths, outside of which were promenading in all their faded grandeur Geordie Henderson as "Richard III."; Lang Lowrie, one of the best men on the stage at a back fall; Wee Perrie, the original "Dumb Man of Manchester"; Johnnie Burnie, the Irish comedian, flourishing his shillelagh.

Bill Adams, a man of many parts, had a panorama painted of George Cruickshanks' picture of "The Bottle," but was interdicted from exhibiting it. Next week was the Fair. His booth was up. What was he to do for an attraction? He hit on an idea, and going to Wombwell's Show he borrowed a fox, a monkey, and some other beasts and birds.

My friend and I were visiting the shows, and seeing an intimation painted up inviting the public to come and see "the happy family," we paid our pennies and entered. Walking round a big cage was Bill Adams, calling out, "Ladies and gentlemen, here are these wild animals, which are natural foes, living together here in harmony for weeks, ay, months."

Suddenly there was a flutter and a quack. The fox had the duck by the neck, and Bill was laying on the fox with a stick, shouting, "You brute, this is the third duck you have killed this week."

# CHAPTER V.

### THE BREAD RIOTS.

IN the preceding chapter I have tried to picture the Saltmarket in its gay, jaunty, holiday aspect, as it appeared at the time of the Fair.

But I have seen the old Saltmarket in a very different mood. I have seen it swept with a tumultuous crowd of angry men, with passion blazing in their eyes, and revolution filling their hearts—men rendered desperate by hunger and want, and burning with a sense of wrong. I have seen it when the forces of law and order were completely subverted, and when for forty-eight hours robbery and anarchy prevailed in the town.

I can well remember the Bread Riots in Glasgow. They took place in the year 1848. By this time I was making a good business as a wood engraver, had married, and was living in the Gallowgate.

It was a time of great distress all over the country. Provisions were dear. Bread was selling at elevenpence for the quartern loaf, and potatoes cost a

## A Period of Distress.

shilling a stone. It was just after the potato famine and before the repeal of the Corn Laws. The number of unemployed was very great. A wave of commercial depression was passing over the land. The weaving trade, which was still one of the staple industries of the West of Scotland, was going down before the introduction of the power-loom. My father, who saw how things were going, sold off his weaving shop and cottage in Paisley, and came to Glasgow, where he started in business as a stationer, bookseller, and librarian at 25 George Street, being one of the first to start a circulating library in Glasgow.

The majority of the weavers, however, were not in a position to turn to other employments. They attributed the prevailing distress to misgovernment. The Chartist agitation, which was revolutionary in its methods, found ready support among the hungry artisans. The spirit of revolt was abroad everywhere.

Such was the feeling of the country in the spring of 1848. In order to alleviate the distress in Glasgow, soup kitchens were established and distributions of meal to the starving weavers were undertaken. These measures proved inadequate, and the cry "Give us bread," was frequently heard.

Many of the recipients of these doles also regarded this as adding insult to injury—giving them charity in place of work and wages.

The events of that March afternoon, when the seething discontent of the weavers burst all bounds, are still graven in my memory.

I had a good opportunity of knowing what the feelings of the unemployed were, for the Town Council had rented a hall just above my house in the Gallowgate as a meeting-place and recreation-room for those out of work. Day by day this hall was filled with discontented, despairing men who had a contempt for the methods of relief adopted by the Corporation. But on the day when the riots broke out—Monday, 6th March, 1848—the forenoon was quiet, and gave no presage of the coming storm.

Soon after the midday meal a great gathering of the unemployed was held at the Nelson Monument at the Green, a spot where many a stirring speech has been made. Here addresses were delivered of a very inflammatory kind. One of the speakers urged his hearers to do "a deed worthy of France," a phrase which will be understood when it is remembered that France was then in the throes of a revolution. It was resolved by those assembled that they should send a deputation to the City Hall to demand bread or work.

Accordingly, off they went in large numbers to the City Hall, where the members of the Town Council were sitting in conclave discussing the unsettled condition of the town. The deputation marched to the Council Chamber and laid their demands before the City Fathers. The answer they got was held to be very unsatisfactory. The Councillors said that nothing more could be done, as the Lord Provost was then absent, but they were arranging for another distribution of food.

"We want something better than that, and we mean to have it," was the reply of the deputation, which then marched back to the Green. Here the reply of the Town Council was given, and the meeting resolved to take for themselves what they could not get by other means.

The mob accordingly dispersed in bands. One of these came up John Street and broke into the first provision shop on the way. Another went down Great Hamilton Street. Some made as if they were going to destroy the Gasworks, and others tried to bring out the whole of the weavers in Bridgeton, and to order a general strike. In this they failed, but for many days the mills had to be carefully guarded by officials and workmen.

One grocer doing an extensive business in the east end adopted a smart device. As soon as he heard that the rioters were coming he shut up shop, and stuck a bill over his shutters announcing "Shop to Let." The looters, thinking the place was empty, passed on. Meeting a bread van in the street, the leaders stopped it, and threw all the bread into the street, where it was picked up by the hungry rioters.

An attack was made on the shop of Mrs. Musgrove, situated near the Tron Steeple. It was a big ironmongery establishment, where a considerable number of guns and other firearms were kept for sale. Mrs. Musgrove offered some resistance to the raiders, but she was promptly bundled out into the street through the shop window.

Brandishing the guns they had taken, and firing shots indiscriminately into the air, the mob passed on westward, breaking windows and looting shops of all kinds of goods. The bakers' and provision shops suffered most, but even tailors' and jewellers' establishments were pillaged.

On they surged to Exchange Square, where the shop of Martin, the gunmaker, was despoiled and more guns taken. Some Buchanan Street shops were broken into and articles of jewellery stolen. By four o'clock in the afternoon the city, which an hour before had been perfectly quiet, was in a state of siege. The greatest excitement prevailed.

Word was at once sent along to the infantry barracks in the Gallowgate and to the cavalry barracks in Eglinton Street asking for the assistance of troops to quell the rising, but owing to the formalities which required to be gone through some time elapsed before the military arrived.

About five o'clock in the afternoon a squadron of cavalry came riding along the street. The rioters were still at their work, but as soon as they caught sight of the redcoats they dropped guns and pistols, and made off. A considerable quantity of stolen property was thus recovered.

I remember when the cavalry were coming along the Trongate, a lot of rowdies took up a position in the Rob Roy Close, which they barricaded with boards and shutters, and from that position they kept up a fusillade on the military. When the police and troops charged them, the rowdies rushed upstairs to the top of the houses and on to the roofs, from which they threw down missiles on the police.

Soon after the cavalry appeared on the scene a strong detachment of infantry marched along the Gallowgate from the infantry barracks, which were located where is now a great railway goods terminus.

The soldiers marched along the Gallowgate, dispersing the mob and dispossessing them of their stolen goods. The Gallowgate was lined with men and women, and the soldiers had to run the gauntlet of blows from fists and sticks. They marched steadily on, however, intent on clearing away the rioters.

As disorder was rife in the Gorbals district, the infantry marched down the Saltmarket and across the Bridge into that quarter, and for some time paraded the thoroughfares of the southern suburb.

The cavalry patrolled the streets in the centre of the city, escorting Bailie Stewart, who read the Riot Act wherever a crowd was assembled. In the Saltmarket and High Street the throng was so great that the cavalry had to make several charges in order to disperse the people.

But as the crowds gave way in one place they assembled in another. Numerous arrests were made, among those captured being one fellow who made himself conspicuous by walking in front of the procession vigorously ringing a bell.

THE BREAD RIOTS, 1848.

## Suppressing the Outbreak.

Amid such scenes of disorder night closed in—a night of fear and uncertainty, the outcome of which no man could foretell. To many in Glasgow the deeds of that day were regarded as the first blows struck for freedom and for the People's Charter. They considered that they were helping to inaugurate a new era—an era of liberty, equality, and fraternity.

Prompt measures were, however, taken by the authorities for the suppression of the disorder. A proclamation was at once issued by the Magistrates, asking all well-disposed citizens to meet that night in St. George's Parish Church, to be sworn in as special constables. This was followed by another proclamation, asking all the people who were not going to enroll as special constables to retire to their homes. Later in the evening, this was followed by a third proclamation, intimating that the Riot Act had been read, and imploring all good citizens to return to their houses.

There was little sleep in Glasgow that night. A large number of the citizens loyally turned out to take the oath to defend the city against the elements of lawlessness. By eight o'clock at night, parties of special constables and military were stationed in High Street, Saltmarket, Trongate, and Gallowgate.

At the Cross, and here and there in the Trongate, at the head of the Saltmarket and High Street, fires were kindled in the streets to give light to the military and police, and to enable them to keep the streets clear. From my windows I could see them parading the thoroughfare and moving on the parties of rioters who remained abroad.

All through the night there was the sound of conflict—the tumult and the shouting—as the military charged the rioters. Every now and then was heard the crash of breaking glass, which told that another of the street lamps had been destroyed. When morning broke scarcely a lamp remained in Gallowgate, High Street, and Duke Street.

Anticipating a renewal of the disturbance on Tuesday, the city authorities sent word to Hamilton for additional troops. Early in the morning they came prancing along London Road. A warm reception was prepared for them by the rioters. Barricades were thrown across the street to impede their progress.

I soon found that my house was in a dangerous quarter. The hall above, which was used as a recreation room by the unemployed, was occupied by a force of the rioters well armed with stones and other missiles, which they discharged from the

## A Tragic Incident.

windows at the soldiers as soon as they came within range. I concluded that it was time for me to get my wife and child to a place of safety, and accordingly we left the building just as the soldiers were coming to evict the rioters.

A serious conflict took place in another part of the town. Mr. Smart, who was assistant superintendent of the Calton police, and afterwards for many years head of the whole of the Glasgow force, was on Tuesday morning conveying a prisoner to the Calton Police Office. He had with him a small body of pensioners, or "old fogies," as we called them, who were armed with muskets loaded with ball. The sight of the prisoner roused the fury of the mob.

Hooting and groaning was indulged in, and then stones were thrown. Mr. Smart and many of the pensioners were struck, and as the party approached Main Street, Bridgeton, the aspect of the mob became very threatening. At this juncture Mr. Smart gave the order to the force under him to charge the crowd. The muskets were levelled and a volley was fired into the rioters with fatal effect.

One man dropped dead on the spot shot through the head, another was wounded in the breast and died the following day, while three others were wounded, two of them so seriously that they also succumbed to their injuries. The most unfortunate circumstance about the affair was that it was not the rioters who suffered. The man Carruth who was shot dead was inoffensively standing at his shop door, while another man who was fatally wounded had been acting as a special constable.

This lamentable occurrence added fuel to the wrath of the rioters. Placing the dead body of Carruth on a shutter they carried it shoulder-high through the streets, a vast crowd following, loudly demanding vengeance for this outrage. It was well that there was so strong a detachment of soldiers in the town by this time.

I can recall, as if it were yesterday, the arrival of that yelling mob as it swept along towards the Cross, bearing its ghastly burden in front. Hearing the tumult, the officer in charge of the infantry stationed at the Tontine turned his men out, and drew them up across the Trongate, preventing the progress of the rioters westward.

Those who were carrying the body marched right up to the points of the bayonets, but the glitter of cold steel cowed them. Disregarding the shouts of the rabble behind, who urged them to go forward in spite of the soldiers, they listened to the expostulations of the officers in command, and gave an attentive ear to Sheriff Bell, who, from the pedestal of King William's statue, read the Riot Act, and advised them to return quietly to their homes. The body of Carruth was conveyed to the Central Police Office, and the crowd soon dispersed.

Thus ended the Bread Riots. Distress and discontent prevailed for some time, and the memories of those terrible events lingered long in the Calton. Several persons were punished for their part in looting. One young man was transported for having been found in possession of a pistol. Another youth, however, who had been taking a hand in pillage afterwards became conscience-stricken, and returned to Mrs. Musgrove a packet of razors to which he had helped himself in the "skirl," as the attack was called. He accompanied his restitution with a bit of rhyme :—

> "Kind mem or sir I'll no deny't
> I took your razors at the riot,
> But noo since things hiv a' turned quiet,
>     At lang an' last,
> Your articles to you I've hied
>     Wi' muckle haste."

# CHAPTER VI.

### THE FIRST ROYAL VISIT TO GLASGOW.

THE year after the occurrence of the events recorded in the previous chapter was marked by several incidents of more than ordinary importance. It was in that year—1849—that Queen Victoria paid her first visit to Glasgow, and was accorded a hearty welcome from the loyal citizens of St. Mungo. The year was also marked by one of the greatest disasters in the annals of the city.

The visit paid by Queen Victoria and the Royal Family in August, 1849, was not the first they had made to the West of Scotland. In the previous summer they toured through some of the finest scenery of the West Highlands, and landed at Dumbarton. I remember the event well, for I went down by boat specially to make sketches of the visit. The ancient town was gaily decorated as the Queen and Prince Albert passed through it. They had been visiting Loch Lomond, and rejoined the Royal yacht at Dumbarton.

This was the first time I had had a chance of seeing the Queen or the Prince Consort. The Queen was then young, slim, and girlish-looking. Prince Albert was a fine, manly fellow. The crowds cheered and the Queen and Prince bowed and smiled their acknowledgments. I kept my pencil going taking sketches which I afterwards published in a broadside along with a description of the ceremony.

But the visit to Glasgow in the following year was a much more pretentious affair. It was made by sea, for the railway systems of the country were then in their infancy.

Queen Victoria and Prince Albert, along with the Royal children, were making a tour of the country. They came to the West of Scotland from the North of Ireland where they had been paying a visit to Belfast. The Royal yacht sailed up to Arrochar at the head of Loch Long.

The original intention was that the Queen and Prince Consort should drive across the narrow neck of land between Arrochar and Tarbert at the head of Loch Lomond and sail down that beautiful stretch of water. But the weather was not of the best and the Queen was not inclined to give up the comfort of the Royal yacht for the inferior accommodation of a loch steamer. Prince Albert accordingly sailed alone down the loch to Balloch and then proceeded to Dumbarton, where he joined the Royal yacht that had come down from Arrochar.

Next day was a gala day in Glasgow. It was regarded as a general holiday. All who possibly could ceased work for the day. Along the line of procession dense crowds assembled, all eager to see the Royal party. I made a picture of the procession, as I knew what it would be like, using the sketches I made of the Queen and Prince Consort at Dumbarton on the previous year. My father got this printed along with the description of the route of the procession and sold as a penny broadsheet.

The sheets went like hot cakes, for, whatever discontent there might have been a year ago, there was now certainly nothing but the friendliest and most loyal feelings towards the members of the Royal house.

The Queen, Prince Albert, and their children left the Royal yacht, and embarked on the steamer *Fairy*, which, escorted by three other river steamers, proceeded slowly up the river. All along the banks were cheering crowds. Clydebank, that great hive of industry, had not sprung into existence yet, but, on the opposite bank, Renfrew was exuberantly gay. Mottoes were displayed, and banners were hung out

# Landing at Kingston Dock.

everywhere. "Hurrah for V. A. and the bairns" was one of the best.

The people crowded down to the water's edge, and, when the *Fairy* passed, the wave swept along gave many of them wet feet, to the evident amusement of the young Prince of Wales, the present King, then but a mischievous laddie of about eight years old.

At last the Royal party arrived at Kingston Dock, and disembarked opposite West Street. Great preparations had been made by the town to give the Queen a fitting welcome, and a triumphal arch was erected at the north end of Jamaica Bridge.

Old "Hawkie" was standing viewing the arch on that day, when a man accosted him with—"Well, 'Hawkie,' what do you think the height of that arch will be?" "The height of nonsense," was "Hawkie's" retort.

The procession then formed, and slowly wended its way through the streets. Over the Broomielaw Bridge it marched, and then along Jamaica Street, Argyle Street, Queen Street, George Street, Duke Street to the Cathedral; then down by the University to High Street, and back to Queen Street Station, where the party entrained for Edinburgh.

Platforms were erected here and there along the

route, and seats were let out at fairly good prices. Many of the shopkeepers were enterprising enough to let out seats in their windows for the purpose of viewing the procession.

Saturday, 17th July, 1849, was a night of wailing in Glasgow such as the city has, fortunately, seldom experienced. One of those heartrending catastrophies that every now and then occur took place in the old Theatre Royal in Dunlop Street. A drama entitled "The Surrender of Calais" was being performed, and at the close of the first act a slight outbreak of fire was observed near a gaspipe in one of the upper galleries. One of the attendants promptly extinguished the flames with his cap, but the audience was alarmed by the cry of "Fire!"

Those who were in a position to see assured the audience that there was no cause for alarm, but this was not heeded, and the appearance of a fireman to examine the place where the outbreak had occurred was the signal for a panic.

The theatre was crowded, there being some five hundred persons in the upper gallery. They were for the most part young lads and girls of the poorer class, attracted by the low prices, for the gallery seats on that night cost only threepence. The gallery was reached by a narrow stone stair leading

## Disaster in the Theatre Royal.

down to the street. A few steps up from the entrance was a pay-box.

Down rushed the panic-stricken crowd pell-mell to gain the street. The foremost of them had reached the landing at the pay-box, and a few steps more would have taken them to the open air, when one tripped and fell on the landing. In a moment he was buried beneath on avalanche of humanity. That stair soon became a fearful pit of death. There was no escape for those in front. Hundreds of struggling human beings behind, madly endeavouring to force a passage to the open air, soon crushed the life out of the unfortunates who were packed on the landing at the pay-box.

The fire brigade had been summoned to put out the fire, but, finding there was no need for their services, the men were returning to headquarters when they were told of the terrible struggle going on in the staircase. They returned at once, but found it was impossible to attempt to extricate any by the door, so firmly were the poor victims wedged together. The firemen put their ladders against the wall, and wrenched away the iron stanchions of the staircase windows, meaning to try to rescue some through that aperture. The windows, however, were too small.

Mr. Alexander, the manager of the theatre, was on the stage when he was told that there was a fight for life on the gallery stair. He at once hurried to the spot, and, though he was clad in armour, he made desperate efforts to rescue those in danger. Fifty by his efforts were extricated from their perilous plight, and conveyed down by the stage door. By and by the panic subsided, and the weary, gasping crowd came back from the pit of death on the stair.

The house that had a quarter of an hour before been full of mirth and gaiety was now a charnel house, in which tragedy in downright, grim earnest reigned supreme. In all, no fewer than sixty-five persons lost their lives on that terrible night.

They were mostly young people, apprentice lads and lasses who had not long left school. Most pitiful case of all was that of one tiny victim—a little girl three years of age.

This disaster cast a gloom over many a family in Glasgow. In one home there were three blanks caused by the tragedy, a mother being bereaved of three sons.

Everything that possibly could be done to make reparation was attempted. No one felt the effect of it more than poor Alexander, the manager of the theatre. Some said that it broke his heart. I know that he was never the same after the occurrence.

In connection with the Royal visit, I should mention that Queen Street Station, from which the Queen and Royal Family departed, was the first station within the city. It was then a small place. I have a distinct recollection of the days before such a station existed. The site was occupied by the mansion-house of James Ewing of Strathleven, a successful merchant, who was popularly known as "Craw Jamie." In the trees about his house there nested, year after year, a colony of particularly noisy rooks. Hence the nickname bestowed on the merchant prince.

The ground between this house and the old City Poorhouse in Parliamentary Road—the Asylum it was then—contained a large number of pig-styes. I remember seeing also the remains of Harley's byres at the corner of Bath Street and West Nile Street. At the corner of George Street and Dundas Street stood the church of Dr. Wardlaw, one of the most popular preachers of the day. It now forms part of the railway offices. There were no other houses until one came to the Cowcaddens.

When Queen Street Station was built, it was then almost in the suburbs. The enormous Central

Station, with its 600 trains daily and its seventeen million passengers yearly, was not then dreamt of. Both the Caledonian and the Glasgow and South-Western Railway ran their trains into a common station on the south side of the river—now the disused Bridge Street Station. When at last the Glasgow and South-Western Railway crossed the Clyde, and built the huge terminus in St. Enoch Square, it was declared by some that this immense station would serve the needs of all the three Companies.

Let me try to give you some idea of the appearance of the Clyde as it was sixty or more years ago. Standing on the old Broomielaw Bridge and looking over to the south-west, nothing was to be seen but green fields. On the west side of the Bridge there was what was known as the "weir"—a great dam which was constructed by tilting over some thousands of cartloads of stones into the stream to protect the foundations of the old bridge from the wearing action of the current. This barrier raised the level of the Clyde by some five feet. In the summer time, boys might be seen standing on the barrier fishing for braise or eels. No wharves then lined the Clyde, but a long row of stone steps led down from the green fields to where lay the small wherries bearing herrings from Loch Fyne or fruit from a French or Spanish port, or brushwood for making besoms from some Highland village. Looking along towards the Green, the first conspicuous object was the big red cone of the glasswork, which stood exactly where the custom-house now is. Along the road facing the Clyde was also a ropework, the first in the city, which extended as far east as Ropework Lane. Then came the Roman Catholic Chapel, on the site of which is St. Andrew's Cathedral, beside which stood the old City Poorhouse. At the foot of Stockwell Street stood the mansion-house of "Bob Dragon," as Mr. Robert Dreghorn was called in his day. He was long since dead, but his memory is kept as that of the ugliest man of his time in the city, and the greatest libertine. Further east of this mansion-house is the Jail, and then the Green, stretching away along the banks of the Clyde as far as Rutherglen Bridge.

On the south bank of the Clyde there were few buildings of any consequence with the exception of Higginbotham's Mill. On entering the Green one of the first buildings you saw was the "dead house," not far from Arn's Well. It was, and is still, the headquarters of the Humane Society, and was for long used as a mortuary. It was looked after by Geordie Geddes, father of the present "rescue." Geordie had then a large number of boats for hire. The river was a gay place on Saturday afternoons, for the boat clubs were generally practising, and races were of frequent occurrence. It was also a favourite diversion for the young sparks of the time to take their sweethearts to Rutherglen by boat. They generally landed near the pleasure gardens of Bauldy Baird, where they got refreshments of curds and cream or strawberries. These were served in a summer-house in the garden, and from this temperate feast the excursionists returned by boat to the city healthier and happier than when they left. On the north bank of the Clyde there was a number of spring-boards used by the bathers. The boards were about eighteen feet long, and six or seven feet above the water. It was a fine sight on a summer evening or Sunday morning to see scores of young men plunging into the water from these diving-boards and swimming about. On both sides of the Clyde at the Green were trees growing—beeches, Scotch firs, and saughs. The Green was much more picturesque than it is now. It was finely diversified with trees and grassy hollows. The "lassies liltin' ower the pail" had not disappeared, for washings were still done at the

Green, and there was always to be seen some girls washing or rinsing their clothes at the Molendinar Burn, which flowed through the Green and into the Clyde at the foot of Saltmarket. There were still cows grazing on a part of the Green. Women milked them and sold the milk in "tinnies" to the people frequenting this the only public park. Round Arn's Well, a famous pump which has disappeared, there was always to be seen a large number of women waiting to get their stoups filled.

There was in those days a somewhat strange character named "Thomas the Rhymer," whose sayings and prophecies were much quoted. I remember two of his prophecies were fulfilled in a rather unexpected fashion. He predicted that the Clyde would come up to the Rotten Row, a part of the High Street that stands considerably above the level of the streets nearer the river. When the East End waterworks were started the reservoir was put down there. The water was taken from the Clyde, and thus "Thomas the Rhymer's" prophecy came to pass.

Thomas also predicted that lion cubs would be born on the Green. To many this seemed a vision of coming desolation, but the fulfilment was harmless enough, and did not interfere with the prophet's veracity nor with the prosperity of the city. When Wombwell's menagerie visited the city during the holidays one year it encamped on the Green, and a lioness actually gave birth to cubs.

# CHAPTER VII.

### SOME GLASGOW CLUBS.

SIXTY years ago Glasgow was much better provided with clubs than it is to-day. There was one in almost every tavern, and many interesting characters were to be met in them. I was an enthusiastic clubman myself, and my business brought me into contact with a number of the members of these convivial associations.

One of the brightest of these clubs was named the Garrick. As may be imagined, it was associated with the stage. The members met in M'Laren's Tavern, opposite the old Theatre Royal in Dunlop Street, the site of which is now occupied by part of St. Enoch Station.

The members of the Garrick were mostly drawn from the theatrical profession and the regular patrons of the theatre. In those days the Theatre Royal was not supplied by travelling companies, but Mr. Alexander had a stock company attached to the theatre. The actors were then much more identified with the life of the town than now, when they only come on flying visits.

Miller's Adelphi Theatre, at the Saltmarket, was supplied with touring companies, and there was never any lack of new faces at the Garrick Club. The scene was ever changing, as the star was there the one night and the strolling player the next. At the head of the table was John Mann, the inventor of many of the tricks performed by Anderson, the famous conjuror, who earned the title, "The Wizard of the North." Among other habitues were Old Fitzroy, the "Uncle Tom" of his day; handsome George Ewing, the sculptor of Burns' Monument, and a son of the proprietor of Ewing's Waxwork; Little Lloyd, one of the favourite comedians, who sipped his whisky punch as if he did not owe a penny in the world, which was generally far from being the case; Johnny Burnie, the Irish comedian; jolly George Webster, who acted the part of Dandie Dinmont; and Tom Powrie, the Fitzjames of the "Lady of the Lake." Here might also have been seen Mossman, the sculptor, and his young friend, Sam Bough, then a scene painter, afterwards the famous artist. It was here also that I last met Gustavus Brooke, the famous tragedian, shortly before his death at sea by shipwreck.

# John Henry Alexander.

I have vivid recollections of old Alexander, the proprietor of the Theatre Royal. Like all the managers of that time, and like his illustrious namesake and many others of to-day, he was an actor as well as manager. In his youth he was a fine-looking fellow, standing almost six feet in height, and of athletic build. He was a good actor, and was very popular in Glasgow. He had a step dance which was much in demand, especially among the "gods," who would insist on "Alick's step," as they called it, being gone through at the most inappropriate times, as the following incident will show:

"Romeo and Juliet" was being played, and Mr. Alexander was to take the part of Romeo, the youthful lover. As he was then an old man of seventy, there was some curiosity to see how he would perform the part. All went well till they came to the love scene. Romeo was cooing lovingly to Juliet, and was going to kiss her, when the ludicrous nature of the proceeding dawned on Juliet. The spectacle of an old man with nose and chin almost meeting playing the part of an ardent young lover made Juliet burst into a loud laugh. The audience roared, and laughter and cheering prevailed for some time. The gods yelled and shouted for Alick's step dance, which had to be gone through before they would allow the play to proceed.

Another anecdote of old Alexander may be here told. On one occasion a boy had got into the theatre in the usual way by paying his sixpence. When the interval came he wanted to go out to parade before some of his less fortunate companions who were hanging about the door. The checktaker, however, was in a difficulty, as his supply of pass-out checks had become exhausted.

"I'll tell you what," he said, "I'll put a chalk mark on your back, and that will admit you."

The mark was accordingly made on the lad's back. When the time for the curtain rising came, and the house began to fill up again, the bewildered checktaker noticed about a score of boys with chalk marks on their backs marching in. He smelt a rat, and the next lad who tried to pass in on the strength of a chalk mark was unceremoniously kicked downstairs. It happened, however, that this was the only lad who had a claim to be admitted, and accordingly his father in wrath called on Mr. Alexander to complain. The actor-manager pacified the man, and afterwards gave a word of caution to the checktaker.

John Henry Anderson, "the Wizard of the

North," was one of the most famous conjurers that ever performed in a theatre. He used to appear in the halls of the city, and then he built for himself a theatre at the Green, in Jail Square, which was then the great centre for shows in the city. It was situated near the river, on the south side of the Square. It was burned down within twelve or fifteen months, and was never rebuilt.

A man of good appearance and marvellous dexterity, Anderson held his audience spell-bound, and his theatre was always well patronised. He used to exhibit a galvanic battery on the stage, and give shocks with it to any who cared to go and try it. Those who did so were generally glad to drop the handles as soon as they could.

One night a soldier swaggered on to the stage bragging that he would not let go. He gripped the handles, and Anderson switched on an extra strong current. In a moment the warrior was lying on his back on the stage, the next he had jumped over the heads of the orchestra into the stalls, and, turning on the Wizard, he shook his fist in speechless wrath. The audience hugely enjoyed his discomfiture.

John Mann, who is credited with having invented many of the tricks performed by Mr. Anderson, was a well-known Glasgow character. He was a sort of universal genius. Having a shop at the head of the Stockwell, he repaired anything or everything, musical boxes being a specialty. Many of the tricks done by Anderson depended for their effect on mechanical contrivances, and these were invented by Mann. In his theatre the Wizard had dramatic performances as well as his tricks of legerdemain. During the off season he toured the country.

Before leaving the " Wizard of the North," I may mention another character who had a " geggie " not far from Anderson's theatre. This was a man named Scott, who was commonly known as " Cheek and a Half." He used to do the gun trick in his show, allowing himself to be shot at with a gun that purported to be loaded. One night a half-tipsy sailor dropped a button down the muzzle of the gun. Scott was struck on the cheek, and part of it was carried away. He contented himself with managing his " geggie " after that. John Henry Anderson married the daughter of this old showman.

The City or Burns Club met in the Bank Tavern, Trongate, which was owned by Mr. M'Neil, one of the men who had been transported for having taken part in the cotton-spinners' strike in 1837. When he returned to Glasgow after undergoing his sentence, his friends subscribed and acquired this tavern for him. He was getting to be an old man when I knew him.

The Burns Club was composed of all the leading literary men of the city. There you might meet John Craig, the geologist and compiler of Ogilvie's *Dictionary*, surnamed the "Old Fossil"; W. C. Pattison, publisher of the *Practical Mechanics' Magazine*; William Miller, the poet laureate of the nursery; Robert Buchanan, editor of the *Glasgow Sentinel*, and father of the poet of that name; William Cameron, writer of "Morag's Fairy Glen" and other songs; Hugh Macdonald, the author of *Rambles Round Glasgow*; John Kelso Hunter, the cobbler artist; and many others.

I knew William Miller, the Parkhead poet, very well. He was a tall, delicate-looking man, and as gentle as a lamb. He was a wood-turner to trade, and in his best days no one could equal him at his business. He will go down to posterity as the author of that matchless song of childhood—

### "WEE WILLIE WINKIE.

" Wee Willie Winkie rins thro' the toun,
　Upstairs and doonstairs in his nicht goon,
　Tirlin' at the window, cryin' at the lock,
　'Are the weans a' in their bed, for it's noo ten o'clock?'

" Hey, Willie Winkie, are ye comin' ben?
　The cat's singin' grey thrums to the sleepin' hen,
　The dog's speldered on the floor, and disna gie a cheep;
　But here's a waukrife laddie that winna fa' asleep.

" Onything but sleep, you rogue! glowerin' like the moon,
　Rattlin' in an airn jug wi' an airn spoon,
　Rumbling, tumbling roon aboot, crawin' like a cock,
　Skirlin' like I kenna what, waukening sleeping folk.

" Wearied is the mither that has a stoorie wean,
　A wee, stumpie stoussie that canna rin his lane;
　That has a battle aye wi' sleep before he'll close an e'e,
　But ae kiss frae aff his rosy lips gie's strength anew to me."

I had a special interest in Wee Willie Winkie, for the baby hero of that song afterwards became one of my apprentices. He was a smart lad, and after he left me he started in business for himself in Glasgow as a wood engraver, and built up a fine connection.

In the corner of the club might have been seen George Brown, an animal painter, who made a specialty of painting cows, and from that was familiarly known as "Coo Broon." He was a

## Jock Goudie's Tavern.

simple, eccentric character, and might often have been seen in the street with a circle of girls dancing about him, he leading off in singing, "Here we go round by jingo ring."

I once saw him in the Gallowgate sketching the head of an ass, his hands ever lifting up the animal's head while he shouted, "Head up! head up, you donkey!" For some time he occasionally worked for me, and I allowed him the use of a corner in my workshop for a studio, and here he painted many of his pictures.

There were then in the city several pugilistic or sporting clubs. One of these met in the Zebra Tavern at the foot of High Street. Jock Goudie, the prizefighter, was the proprietor of this place, which was the rendezvous of all the sporting men in the city and country around. Not a bad sort was Jock, although a professional pugilist. Indeed, he was a cut above the majority of his customers. I did not take much interest in sporting matters then, nor have I done so since, but I could scarcely avoid knowing about the ongoings in Jock Goudie's tavern, for when I lived in Gallowgate my back windows commanded a view of the back court of the Zebra.

Prize-fighting was then very common in Glasgow. Scarcely a week passed without some contest for stakes being decided. The police did not interfere. The back court of the Zebra was too small for a big encounter. These took place in the fields outside the city, but sparring matches were of daily occurrence, and I used to see Jock daily instructing his pupils in the noble art of self-defence. I knew by the crowds at the tavern when any big encounter was on, for all the sporting fraternity congregated to get the result of the fight.

Many of the smaller taverns in the city at that time had cock-pits and rat-pits in the back courts. Dog fights and cock fights were frequently held, and ratting with terriers was a favourite sport. But Jock Goudie's tavern was the favourite resort of the leading patrons of sport in the West of Scotland.

Here might have been seen the Duke of Hamilton, a tall, dark, thin man; James Merry, the ironmaster, one of the founders of the firm of Merry & Cuninghame, and always attended by his satellite, Norman Buchanan; Lord Kelburne, with his strange *protegé*, Rab 'Ha', the notorious glutton; Ramsay of Barrington, a famous whip, whose love for the ribbons led him to drive the four-in-hand coach between Glasgow and Stirling; and Rab Steel, the marrying Provost of Rutherglen.

The last was a strange character. For several

years he was Provost of the burgh of Rutherglen, which was then at a considerable distance from Glasgow, and a favourite resort of the lads and lasses of the city, who walked out on Sundays and on fine evenings.

Rab was a tollkeeper—I think the house he occupied is still standing—but he was better known in those days for conducting irregular marriages. He did a business something like that of the Gretna Green blacksmith, and he is said to have united more couples than any other individual, except Principal Macfarlane, of the College, whose test of fitness for the holy bond was ability to repeat the Lord's Prayer.

Rab Steel was favoured, because with him the ceremony was delightfully simple and inexpensive. It cost the parties nothing, and there was no searching cross-examination. If a young lad and lass came to the toll and intimated that they desired to be married, Rab simply proclaimed them there and then man and wife and sent them away.

He did not even ask them into the house, nor did he trouble to come out. He simply thrust his head through the window and, addressing the couple on the road, told them it was "A' richt." It was a Scottish marriage of the rough-and-ready type, but it was as binding and as faithfully observed as if it had been performed in a cathedral with the organ pealing the wedding march at the close.

Rab was a short, stumpy man, somewhat like a farmer in build. He was to be seen every market day at the Cross in Glasgow, and usually found his way to Jock Goudie's tavern. I met him frequently when I was living in that quarter.

Goudie had a sad end. He was at Paisley Races, and becoming involved in a scrimmage, was so severely handled by some roughs that he died from the effects of his ill-usage.

One of the oldest taverns in Glasgow stood, or, I should say, still stands, at the head of Maxwell Street. For more than a hundred years M'Culloch's has been a centre of social and literary life in the city. It used to be a great centre of club life half-a-century ago.

Some of these societies still meet there, among them being the Thomas Campbell Club, which is named after the author of *The Pleasures of Hope*. It has a long and honoured career, and, having been founded in the lifetime of the poet, it was presented by him with a cheque for £10, with which a loving cup was bought that for long formed one of the treasured possessions of the club.

## M'Culloch's Tavern.

The Bank Burns Club, which, as I have already mentioned, used to meet in M'Neil's tavern, latterly held its meetings for a long time in M'Culloch's. Among those who used to frequent this old tavern I may mention James Dick, the gutta-percha merchant, who, from the humblest beginnings, built up a great business, and died a millionaire. Another notable personage that I have seen often at M'Culloch's was Bailie James Martin—"Jamie Mairtin," as he was familiarly called in the east end.

Jamie was one of the east end weavers, but when the weaving business went down he started a soft goods warehouse, which his sons still carry on. For a long time he was a member of the Town Council, and no one was better known in the city than he. He was strenuous in fighting against what he considered the abuses of his time. His humorous remarks and eccentricities on the bench were the talk of the town.

Right opposite M'Culloch's tavern was the Bible warehouse of M'Phun, one of the leading booksellers in Glasgow, and just adjoining the tavern was a famous pie-shop occupied by a woman who went by the name of "Pie Nanny." This was also a great resort.

Pie-shops then occupied something the same

position that the tea-rooms do now. The elaborate menus to be seen in the modern restaurants and tea-rooms were then unknown. The favourite lunch consisted of a pie and a pint of porter. On Saturday afternoon and evening that was a luxury which was almost universally enjoyed by certain sections of the citizens.

The pie-shops, which were very numerous in the city, were almost all located below the level of the street. Besides the pie-shop next to M'Culloch's there were numerous others of repute. In Nelson Street and in the vicinity of Bell Street were several old-established shops where pies and porter were in great demand. At almost all the street corners in Gallowgate and Trongate these down-stair pie-shops were to be found.

# CHAPTER VIII.

### PHOTOGRAPHING NOTABILITIES.

AMONG the other notable personalities of half-a-century ago who live in my recollections, may be mentioned Bailie Moir, or, as he was nicknamed, "Rory O'More." He had some of the rollicking humour of Lever's great character, but he had more than that. In the Town Council he held a position of great influence, similar, perhaps, to that occupied by the late Bailie John Ferguson.

When the Chartist movement was spreading in Scotland, he warmly espoused its cause. He was one of the ablest political speakers in Glasgow. A fearless champion of the people's rights, he jealously guarded their old privileges in regard to access to the Green.

When the Town Council, in spite of his strenuous opposition, determined to place restrictions on some of the parts of the Green, he used to go down and dance on the restricted portions, to show that the

Council had no power to enforce the restrictions. The Bailie was a tall, fine-looking man, and had a tea shop in the Gallowgate.

Another notable personality was a grocer in the Gallowgate named Smeal. He was a Quaker, and a strenuous Abolitionist. He was one of the foremost in the agitation that went on in the West of Scotland for the freeing of the slaves in America. The Abolition movement was very strong in Glasgow, and when the Free Church got some £4,000 from America, just after the Disruption, the cry was raised—"Send back the money." It was urged that the money which had been given by slave-holders ought not to be received, and on walls all over the city were plastered posters, bearing the legend, "Send back the money."

There are many in Glasgow who may remember John Anderson, the founder of one of the biggest commercial houses in the city. When I first knew him he had a small drapery establishment in the Gorbals. Then he crossed the water and started business on the west side of Jamaica Street, between Ann Street and the Broomielaw. There were then scarcely any houses west of Jamaica Street until you came out to the village of Anderston, about half a mile distant.

The railway had not crossed the Clyde, and what is now the busiest thoroughfare in Scotland—perhaps in any town out of London—was then a quiet place. John Anderson was a man of culture as well as of business enterprise. He started a waxwork and museum in a building in Jamaica Street that had formerly been occupied by a circus.

In this waxwork there were singing entertainments and scientific lectures, Mr. Anderson bringing some of the ablest scientists of the day to Glasgow to deliver lectures. Mr. Anderson called his hall of science the Polytechnic. It was carried on for a few years, and then he removed to Argyle Street, and went into the drapery business exclusively, retaining the name Polytechnic for his business concern.

When I was in business as a photographer, Mr. Anderson came to my studio with the Rev. C. H. Spurgeon. I photographed the famous Metropolitan preacher, and the results were so pleasing that Mr. Anderson and his distinguished friend came back later and wanted an estimate for a large number of copies. We failed to come to an agreement, my terms being higher than they expected.

I remember the young divine perfectly well. He took an interest in my work, and I tried to explain to him as best I could the mysteries of the photographic art, but he did not seem to grasp them. The great preacher was certainly not a scientist.

I ought at this stage to say something about myself and my business. It had grown rapidly, and in 1849 I had removed from the vicinity of the Zebra Tavern, in the Gallowgate, to 33 Buchanan Street, where I took a two-roomed office. Here I remained for twenty years, extending my premises as my business grew.

Any of my readers who are curious enough to see the place where my business was conducted, will be disappointed. Buchanan Street is not what it was in my time. The palatial shops and enormous warehouses which give that thoroughfare a title to be regarded as the leading street in the city were not then. The street contained a number of old-fashioned, two-storey houses, with crow-stepped gables and outside stairs leading up to the second storeys. These outside stairs were of the familiar double variety, so common in those days, one stair going up to each side of a common landing. The building I was in had belonged to David Dale, the great philanthropist. The Anchor Line Steamship Company had their offices in the wide pend below me, and I used to do some engraving work for them.

My business by this time had grown very largely, and I had five or six apprentices working along with me. I engaged the services of outside artists to make sketches on the blocks of pictures to be engraved. A great part of my work was derived from the *Practical Mechanics' Monthly Journal*. I did the wood engravings from the very commencement of that magazine. This was the biggest and steadiest job that I had; but all the printers now knew me, and gave me work to do. The first editor of the *Practical Mechanics' Journal* was Mr. Buchanan, who afterwards went to be manager of the Fairfield Shipbuilding Yard, which, under the guidance of John Elder, was taking a foremost place in the marine engineering science of the world. Then William Johnston, the patent agent, took it up, and he became proprietor.

This work brought me into contact with all the inventors of Glasgow and neighbourhood, for I had to engrave pictures of their inventions. How many of these so-called inventions proved miserable failures, I should not care to say. Probably the percentage was not any higher than it is now, but many of the machines I had to engrave were palpably ridiculous.

I remember meeting Lord Cromartie, afterwards Duke of Sutherland. He was a young man of about thirty, with a passion for mechanics, which we rarely find in the heir to a dukedom. I met him in Mr. Johnston's house, where he was arranging about some patents he was taking out. I was told then that he had a small engineering shop at Dunrobin Castle. He talked to Mr. Johnston about locomotives, the improvement of the railway engine being his great ambition.

I also met in this way Mr. M'Onie, who afterwards became Lord Provost of Glasgow. He was a very capable engineer, and did much to improve the sugar machinery, of which his firm made large quantities. Napier of Shandon, and his brother, who were then perfecting the marine engine, were also frequent visitors at the house of Mr. Johnston, and I met them there. The two brothers were then in the heydey of their fame as engineers.

I had frequent meetings with John Robertson, the maker of the engines of the *Comet*, the first steamboat that was a practical success. Before this epoch-making engine was taken away to Kensington Museum I took a photograph of it with Robertson standing beside it. This photograph was very frequently reproduced, but is now a rarity.

There was much talk about the great International Exhibition which was to take place in

**JOHN ROBERTSON,**
Maker of the Engine for the *Comet*.

*Page 106.*

# International Exhibition, 1851.

London in 1851, and I determined to go up and see it.

Many a time have I visited London since, both on business and pleasure, but the recollection of that first stay in modern Babylon stands out clear and plain across the intervening half-century and more. I went by rail, for the locomotive had become by this time a great power in the land. The journey did not occupy more than fifteen hours, and the fare was not much more than at present. Special excursions were being run in connection with the Exhibition. I went down with one of these, and stayed three weeks in London.

I was in the Exhibition almost every day, and was greatly impressed with the vastness of the building, the greatness of the crowds that thronged it, and the wonderful variety of the products that were to be seen there. The machinery and the pictures, especially the daguerreotypes, were the principal sources of attraction to me. I met the Duke of Wellington coming out of the Horse Guards, and recognised him at once. He was on horseback, and though white and frail-looking there was no mistaking the tall spare figure and the eagle glance of the hero of a hundred fights. I took off my hat, and the Duke instantly returned the salute. In spite of the fascination which London had for me, I had, however, no desire to settle down in it, and I was glad enough to go back to my work and my home in Glasgow.

But this visit to London had stimulated my interest in the daguerreotype process, and I thought it might be a good thing if I could work it in connection with my wood engraving business. If I could manage to daguerreotype the picture I was engraving on to the wooden block, and then go over it with the graving tool, it would be a much quicker and cheaper process than having each sketch drawn by hand on the block before being engraved.

As I was not able to overtake all the sketching work myself I had to employ outside artists. Among these the most promising was a young lad named Simpson, then an apprentice with Allan & Ferguson. Latterly he went out to the Crimea as representative of the *Illustrated London News*, and won fame as the first of war artists. He was better known as Crimean Simpson. He was an antiquarian as well as an artist, and a fine collection of sketches in water-colours of pictures of old Glasgow executed by him is now in the possession of the Corporation.

The first incident I remember connected with

photography was seeing a daguerreotype, which was shown to me by a friend. The art at that time was thought a very great mystery.

Before the days of the daguerreotypes a very popular form of likeness was the beautiful black profiles, or silhouettes, which were turned out by artists in the city. I remember Frith, the black and white artist, who had his place in Queen Street, used to do numbers of these.

The first place where daguerreotypes were taken or shown in Glasgow was at the Zoological Gardens in New City Road. This forerunner of the present Scottish Zoo was located somewhat further west than the present institution. It was one of the favourite resorts of the citizens, for it was then almost in the country, with green fields around.

Mr. Picken, at the Andersonian Institute, also tried the daguerreotype process, and the several operators in the city followed.

I remember the first time I faced the camera. My patience was sorely tried, for I had to sit on the top of a house in Buchanan Street, with the full glare of the sun in my face, for a quarter of an hour. The operator told me not to move till he came back, as there was somebody in the shop requiring attention. I shall never forget what I suffered during that terrible sitting, but we were rewarded with an excellent likeness.

Then I began to experiment with photography. Having read up all that I could about the process, I got the hold of a cigar box, and, with the eye of a pair of spectacles for a lens, I made my first camera. This was long before the days of elaborate and beautifully-constructed cameras. We had then to feel our way. The early photographers had to do everything for themselves—design their own cameras, and get them made by a joiner or cabinet-maker; prepare their own plates and papers; and mix up their own chemicals for development. The daguerreotype process did not prove a practical success so far as my work was concerned, but when the collodion process was introduced I at once applied it with success.

It was about this time that I first came in contact with Sam Bough, the famous artist. A great, burly, bearded fellow, speaking with a broad Lancashire accent, Sam was a rough diamond—but a diamond he was, and no mistake. There was nothing about him that was not genuine. When I first knew him, he had just given up his job as a scene painter at the theatre, and was painting scenes and doing other pot-boiler work.

But the mark of his genius was on all his pictures, and it was not long after this till his art brought him both fame and fortune. I had frequently seen Sam at the Garrick Club sitting with a pint of beer and a long clay pipe, before I had the opportunity of speaking to him.

Sam had been painting a panorama, entitled "The Overland Mail to India," which was to be exhibited in the City Hall. The man who was to run the show came to me and wanted me to prepare some wood engravings of the scenes for advertisement purposes. I asked him how I was to get them, and he told me to go along to a certain address in Bath Street, and Mr. Bough would let me know how he wanted them done.

I accordingly went up to the address and knocked at the half-open door. The big, cheery voice of Sam bade me enter. On pushing the door open, I saw the floor covered with a piece of canvas. The artist, with a pot of paint in one hand and a brush in the other, was walking over the canvas, giving a swish here and a splash there at what seemed a chaotic mass of paint.

I said, "I am afraid I will spoil your picture." "Not at all," he said. "Come in; you will just give it a little extra effect." I remember afterwards going to the City Hall to see that panorama, and being amazed at the wonderfully fine effect produced by what at close quarters seemed exceedingly rough work.

Once when Sam Bough was painting a scene illustrating the "Lady of the Lake," for the Theatre Royal, Mr. Glover came into the room.

"Sam, Sam, that won't do," he exclaimed.

"Won't it?" answered Sam. "Then how will this do?" and he dashed the pail of whitewash on the picture.

Mr. Glover fled in hot haste, but a few touches of Sam's deft brush turned the mass of whitewash into a foaming cataract.

Sam Bough and I became friends, and years after the incident I have described, Sam came out to stay for a short time with me when I was living at the old Castle of Mugdock. He made many sketches of the old fortress, and he gave me many an invitation to visit him at his Edinburgh home, but circumstances prevented me accepting his hospitality.

He was a remarkably quick worker. I have seen him set up a number of pieces of cardboard, and then go round them, making a dash with his brush at each in succession. In this way he rapidly sketched at the same time half a dozen different pictures, in less time than a ordinary man would have taken to paint one.

# CHAPTER IX.

### ADVANCES IN PHOTOGRAPHY.

AS I have already indicated, I soon saw the immense advantage that photography would be to me in my business. Instead of having to employ an artist to sketch an intricate piece of machinery on the wooden block before it could be engraved, I could now photograph it directly on the wood.

This meant a great saving of time and money, and so I cultivated the photographic art assiduously, and did my best to bring it to perfection.

At first I had no thought of applying it to taking portraits, but so many of my friends came about my rooms wishing to have their portraits taken by this wonderful process, that visions of a new and more lucrative branch of business began to dawn upon me.

There was at this time no professional photographer in the city, though several continued to practise the daguerreotype process, and so I resolved to supply what was evidently a felt want. I got permission from my landlord to build a studio on the roof of my office. I accordingly got a glass house constructed, with a door entering in from the roof and a narrow stair leading up to it from the office where I carried on my engraving business.

Mine was, I think, the second glass studio in the city. There was another in Buchanan Street, belonging to a daguerreotypist. I remember with what degree of awe the children used to stand in the street and watch the mysterious figure of the daguerreotypist moving about in his glass house.

Then I invited the editor of the *Glasgow Herald* to come and see my establishment and see the process of photography. The result was an excellent notice in that paper. The effect was wonderful. On the day after the notice appeared in the *Herald* I could scarcely get into my small office. The two rooms were thronged with visitors, who were anxious to have their portraits taken by the new process. I was most agreeably surprised, but at the same time embarrassed by this success.

I did not want to have my engraving business suffer, and I did not want to disappoint my new customers. Clearly I should have to greatly extend my premises or make a choice between the new business and the old.

In course of time I did both. I added room to room as fast as I could, for the demand for portraits increased with a rush, and then, finding that the care of the two branches of work was too much for me, I turned over the engraving business to a nephew and devoted all my energies to photography.

And how I did work in those days! The financial returns which photography brought me were very great, but they were a small consideration compared with the interest of the study of the art itself. I felt like some traveller in a new country with great tracts of undiscovered territory to explore. As the result of my success, I soon had competitors. One of the earliest of these was a clever young fellow named Stephen Young. Like myself, he came from Paisley, and had been in the printing trade with Mr. Gardner, the well-known bookseller and publisher. Young hit on a smart advertisement, and invited the public to "come and have your picture taken by Young & Sun, and see yourself as ithers see you." The sun, of course, is the photographer's most active partner.

At the outset of my career as a photographer, I met with a somewhat nasty accident. I was making some collodion, and, to get the iodide of potassium dissolved, I put the bottle containing the ether and the alcohol into a pot of hot water on the fire. I was suddenly called away, and when I returned, and bent over to take it off, the entire contents were ejected on to my face and head. The latter was instantly in a blaze, and was soon left in the charred condition of a singed sheep's head.

This unlucky mishap proved a prompt extinguisher to my likeness-taking for a time. I was confined to the house for a week until my hair had time to grow, and as there were no assistant operators to be had in those days I had to put up an intimation at my entrance—" Blown Up—Will be down in a few days."

After I "came down" my business went on increasing so rapidly that I was soon obliged to cover some three blocks with glass houses.

About this period another accident occurred, quite as alarming as the previous one, though not so serious. In making some gun cotton I had placed it before the fire spread out on a paper to dry. A toaster with chops frizzling for supper was there, and to my astonishment I caught sight of my chops and toaster making a somersault in the air. The cotton had exploded, and supper and all were gone. Such were some of the dangers and difficulties of the early days of photography.

In my time I have had English, Irish, and Scottish operators, also French, German, and American artists. The Yankee was too 'cute for me, the German too slow, and the Frenchman too demonstrative. The Cockney could do everything—with his tongue; and an Irishman I had, suddenly terminated his artistic existence by taking an overdose of methylated spirits in the dark room.

During my long career as a photographer I have turned my camera on all classes and conditions of men and women, from the squalling babe to the hoary-headed pilgrim who has all but finished life's journey. There are, indeed, few professions in which one has greater opportunities of studying human nature than that of the photographer.

"Well, sir," said a customer to me one day before taking his place in front of the camera, "you know I am an author, and I want you to make my picture as if I was studying a grand poem." I did my best to please. He chanced to be of the beetle-browed order, and the haze thrown on the lower features by this malformation made him exclaim, "That all arises from study and deep thought."

I have on more occasions that I can think of been

employed to assist in love affairs. Young men and maidens came to me to get their photographs taken to send to their sweethearts, and it was amusing to note how particular they were that the likeness should be the best that could be procured. I believe it is the same now.

A fashionably-dressed young swell once came to me and showed me an advertisement purporting to have been written by a lady anxious to secure a partner in life who " must be amiable, good-looking, and intelligent." As she had an ample fortune at her command, suitors were requested to send in their cartes.

"Now, sir," said my customer, " you understand my case. Put into my face all the virtues there stated, and who knows but I may be in time to win the bride."

I could not help smiling at the fellow's presumption, but I modestly declared that I would give him a picture that his friends would recognise.

On another occasion a well-known professional singer called on me and said—" Now, please observe that I am a professional vocalist, and can command any amount of applause by my flexibility of features and unequalled voice. I wish your picture to convey that idea." My client's estimation of himself was by no means exaggerated, but I had no means of giving him flexible features.

When taking large groups I have often seen interesting traits of character displayed. I remember on one occasion, just after the settlement of the Crimean War, a venerable old man with white flowing locks called with his better half, the very type of a shrewd Scottish matron. Three stalwart sons and a couple of interesting daughters completed the family group. The old lady gave me some glimpses of their history.

"Thae five," said she, "is a' left us oot o' thirteen. Davie, the youngest, was killed when followin' Sir Colin at the Alma, and Johnny, the auldest, left his banes in the backwoods o' America. We're noo married fifty years, an' mony an up and doon we've seen, and I want this pictur afore ony mair are taen awa'."

Before the days of flashlight photography or the use of the electric light, we sometimes had difficulty in convincing customers that their pictures could not be taken at night. One evening, just as darkness was setting in, and we were preparing to leave for the day, a woman with a child in her arms called and wished their portraits taken. One of my assistants told her to call again the following day

# Photographing the Bailie.

as the light was bad, but she was deaf to all remonstrances. A picture she would have. In order to get rid of her the assistant rummaged about and found a picture of a woman with a baby in her arms, which he gave her, and asked her to call again next day. She accordingly went away satisfied.

Next day she came back, and in great wrath threw down the photograph. "That's no' me ava," she exclaimed, "but gey like the wean wi' a different frock on."

The pair were duly photographed, and on receiving a proof, the woman said—"Ay, Bobbie, that's you and me noo."

On one occasion a Bailie and his spouse called, the latter being very proud of the honour lately conferred on her husband. When arranging for the picture being taken, she was very particular as to his badge of office being well displayed. The robe and the massive gold chain and badge having been adjusted and readjusted to her heart's content, she admonished her lord—"Noo, jist look as if you wur on the bench and the Coort a' roond you."

A celebrated bagpiper once wanted to be taken in full Highland costume, with his pipes placed in an attitude as if being played upon. I placed him in position, and told him to assume the expression he desired. When I turned my back to take off the cap of the lens, I was astonished to hear the skirling of the pipes. I hastily turned round to see my brave Highlander marching up and down to the tune of "The Campbells are Comin'." When I remonstrated with him, he indignantly exclaimed— "Tid you thocht I want tae be ta'en stanin' like a pig stookie."

A stylishly-dressed lady once called, accompanied by two beautiful boys, who were as restless as a straw in a gale of wind. After repeated and sometimes fruitless efforts to get them to remain still, I at last got their photographs taken. Then a somewhat ludicrous incident happened. The lady told her little ones that they might play about while she got her picture taken alone.

Thus set at liberty, the urchins speedily found their way into every room of my establishment, and were examining everything they could lay their hands upon. Suddenly there came sounds of a crash from the dark room. On hurrying thither, I found that the youngsters had upset my favourite bath, and were literally dripping all over with the contents. I could not conceal my annoyance from the lady, who did the best she could to repair the mischief her sons had caused. She pulled out her white handkerchief, and set about wiping the fluid from her boys' dresses.

The day was uncommonly hot, and the good lady perspired freely, necessitating the frequent application of the handkerchief to her face to remove the drops. I began to perceive her face assuming a dusky hue, and I thought it best to get the party home as soon as possible. In the afternoon I was called upon by the lady's maid, who, amid increasing confusion, related the terrible disaster that had befallen her mistress. Her face and hands were rapidly becoming black and blue, and her grief was the more intense because she had invited a large party to her house that evening. She had tried soap and water and hard scrubbing to remove the obnoxious colour, but all in vain.

She had accordingly sent to get a remedy from me. From the poisonous nature of the chemicals, I thought it best to go to the house of the lady myself rather than entrust them to the care of a servant. With a little patience and a little care we at last succeeded in getting all the objectionable colour off, and the lady was able to meet her guests without the slightest embarrassment.

I once had an order from the Duke of Montrose to send an artist down to Buchanan Castle to take views of the castle and surroundings. In view of the important nature of the commission I went down myself and spent a few days at the castle, taking photographs, not only of the grounds and cattle, but also of the family and servants. A dark room was provided for me there, where I worked. The young members of the Montrose family were all around me when I was at work, looking through my camera or peering at the dishes in the dark room.

The present Duke was then a smart lad, as was also his elder brother, now dead. Both were very anxious to get into the mystery of photography. The old Duke was a good deal with me. He took me all over the castle and grounds, and pointed out the best views. He also showed me a large oil painting of his great-grandfather standing holding the reins of a charger on which was mounted King Charles the First, also a painting of his grandfather dressed in the robes of the Lord Chancellor, of which I made large photographs.

Soon after this I had a note from the Duke to say that he was to call at my studio in Buchanan Street for the purpose of being photographed. When he came I asked him what sort of a portrait he would like. He said that he wanted to be taken in the same position as I had photographed an old character that hung about Buchanan Castle, and who was a great favourite with the servants and children.

One of my most interesting customers was a young lady of good birth and breeding whose deeds were soon to startle the world. Madeline Smith came twice to my studio to be photographed—once along with her father and mother and the other members of the family to be taken in the customary family group, and on another occasion she came alone. She was a strikingly beautiful girl of about twenty, and though there was then nothing but her personality to attract attention, I could not help remembering her.

I also photographed the Frenchman L'Angelier. He was rather a good-looking fellow, not very tall, but smart and dapper. Madeleine Smith did not come with her lover; indeed, the relations between the pair were then known to only one or two intimate friends.

It was about two or three months after I photographed Madeleine Smith that the sensational denouement took place, which ended in her being placed in the dock on the charge of murder. I can well remember the ferment in the town during that time. The majority of people in Glasgow believed that Madeleine was the victim of the wiles of the Frenchman, and that if any blame lay at her door, she was at anyrate more sinned against than sinning. When the trial was proceeding in Edinburgh, I had a finely executed photograph of Miss Smith displayed in my show-cases. It was a large-sized portrait, measuring fifteen inches by twelve, and I had it beautifully coloured by one of my best artists.

The result was that for many days my show-cases were besieged. The crowd round the case was so great as to block the thoroughfare. I was requested by the police to remove it, but it was too good an advertisement, and I declined to do so, and they could not compel me. But the police paraded up and down the pavement in front of my show-case, keeping back the crowd, and making the footway clear.

Soon after the trial was over I took in the picture, and the excitement caused by the Blythswood Square mystery became a thing of the past.

A few years after these events recorded I met Dr. Pritchard, whose name has since become a synonym for baseness, cruelty, and hypocrisy. At the time I was a member of St. Mark's Masonic Lodge. This was at the beginning of the sixties, and I fancy that Pritchard had not long come to Glasgow when he put in an appearance at the meetings of St. Mark's Lodge.

He had been a member of the craft when he was living in England, and probably thought that cultivating the friendship of the members of St. Mark's would assist him in building up a professional connection. He came regularly to Lodge meetings, and I had frequent opportunities of seeing him.

But we never became intimate as brethren of a Masonic Lodge generally do, for, from the first, I felt a sort of instinctive distrust of the man. I disliked the pompous, boastful speeches he was in the habit of making at Lodge meetings, and the oily suavity of his manners. For a scientific man I thought him rather shallow. He was certainly a braggart of the first water, and, as it proved, an out-and-out liar.

A number of others in the Lodge shared the dislike I felt towards him, but his smooth tongue and insinuating ways prevailed with the majority, and in the year after he came to the Lodge he was appointed Master. He was also admitted a member of the Glasgow Royal Arch Chapter.

The Lodge Master when Pritchard came was Donald Campbell, a well-known worthy, who had his place of business in Buchanan Street. Shortly after this I stopped going to the Masonic meetings, as the increasing cares of my business made it impossible for me to find the necessary time.

Although I had no great regard for Dr. Pritchard, I never thought he was so bad as he turned out to be, and no one was more astonished than I was to learn that he had been arrested at Queen Street Station on a charge of having poisoned his relatives.

Almost all Glasgow turned out to his hanging, but I did not. I had no fondness for gruesome spectacles of that kind, and, though I might have witnessed many an execution since I sketched the scaffold of Dennis Doolan, I never went to the Green to witness the grim tragedies of Jail Square.

Another sanctimonious hypocrite that I met about this time was John Henry Greatrex, the forger, who applied his talents to the making of spurious banknotes, and then led the detectives such a dance across the Atlantic.

He was a tall, good-looking man, and an impressive preacher, taking up his stand on the Green regularly. He was a photographer, for by this time I had a considerable number of competitors in business. Greatrex had his studio first in Hope Street, and then in Sauchiehall Street. I was in his studio on more than one occasion, and remember seeing Jenny Weir, the girl that he induced to elope with him.

In order to impress his customers with his piety, Greatrex had his studio hung round with Scripture texts. He found photographing faces much too slow a way of making money, and took to photographing bank notes instead, and this brought about his ruin.

# CHAPTER X.

### RECOLLECTIONS OF DR. LIVINGSTONE.

THERE are few events in my long experience that I recall with feelings of greater pleasure than my association with Dr. Livingstone, the great explorer. He had just come home from South Africa, and the country was ringing with his exploits. He had been enthusiastically received everywhere, had lectured before scientific societies, was lionised in London, feted and courted and flattered in a way that would have effectually turned the head of a less sensible man than the Blantyre weaver who turned missionary.

He had written a book which amply proved that truth is stranger than fiction. His sober, matter-of-fact story of how he had braved death in a thousand forms in his journeyings through the trackless forests and malaria-stricken swamps of South Africa; how he had suffered from hunger and pestilence, had fought with strange and formidable beasts, and been in danger of his life at the hands of savage men scarcely less formidable, excelled in interest the products of the wildest imagination.

Little wonder that we in Scotland, and especially in the neighbourhood of his native town, felt proud of the weaver lad of Blantyre, who had shown such dauntless courage in overcoming difficulties and facing perils. I had bought a copy of Dr. Livingstone's book, and been fascinated with its charm. When the explorer came north to Scotland as the guest of his old friend, Mr. James Young of Kelly, I felt a strong desire to meet him.

James Young was another Scot who achieved fame and fortune in a different sphere of labour. His father was a joiner in the Gallowgate of Glasgow, and he also worked at the joiner's bench in his youthful days. But the fascination of scientific research laid hold of him, and while working the saw and plane during the day, he spent his evenings studying at the Andersonian College. It was here that he met David Livingstone, and the two kindred spirits formed a strong bond of friendship. Mr. Young was an ardent student of chemistry, and became assistant to Professor Graham, of the Mint. The friendship of the two students was interrupted for a number of years when the missionary spirit drove the weaver lad out to the heathen lands of South Africa. When they met again each had done something to keep his name in remembrance. Livingstone had revealed the secrets of a continent—Young had laid the foundation of an important industry for the country and a colossal fortune for himself by the discovery of the method of extracting paraffin oil from shale.

I remember doing some work for Mr. Young after this. He had been involved in litigation over his patent rights, and was sending certain documents to his lawyers, but before he let them out of his hands, he employed me to photograph them. I remember that he was successful in that lawsuit, and obtained damages to the extent of half-a-crown a gallon on all the oil produced by a rival firm by means of his patent process.

When I met Mr. Young he was the proprietor of an estate near Bathgate. He happened to mention that there were no hares on the estate, and in order to make up for this deficiency I got a dozen caught alive and sent to him from my shootings at Mugdock. A short time after that I again met Mr. Young, when he told me that the miners had killed them all. It was some time after this when he acquired the estate of Kelly.

But to return to Dr. Livingstone. As I have said, I was very anxious to meet him, and, to my great joy, I received an invitation from Mr. Young to come out to his house in Sardinia Terrace, Hillhead, for the purpose of being introduced to the great explorer. I gladly availed myself of the invitation, and along with a brother-in-law of James Young, I went along to Sardinia Terrace.

The house where I had that interview with Livingstone is now occupied by Ex-Bailie William Martin. I shall never forget that meeting. We had nearly two hours' conversation in Mr. Young's drawing-room. Naturally the talk was very much one-sided. We were too eager to learn from the explorer's own lips the story of his wonderful adventures to relate our own commonplace experiences, or to trouble with small talk about the weather or the state of the crops.

Livingstone at this time was a man of about fifty years of age. He was seven years older than I was, but he looked rather more, for the experiences of the last score of years had left their mark on his iron frame. His face was swarthy from exposure to tropical suns, and his hair was grizzled. But the strong lines of his face indicated a man of great determination and possessed of a mind devoid of fear. He spoke quietly and modestly of his own adventures, but enthusiastically of Africa and its future. The cause for which he was afterwards to sacrifice his life was the first and only consideration.

Livingstone's arm was stiff as the result of his encounter with a lion. This and many other adventures he related, which have since been told and re-told again and again, so they need not be recounted here. He had just discovered the wonderful falls of the Zambesi, which he named after the Queen, and he was full of the beauties of that marvellous region.

Mr. Young desired that I should take a photograph for him of Dr. Livingstone, and accordingly an appointment was made. Dr. Livingstone came to my studio in Buchanan Street, and I took his photo. It proved to be an excellent likeness, and has been produced again and again in various books and magazines, for I believe it was the only time the great explorer was photographed alone.

A short time afterwards, at the request of Mr. Young, I took another photo of Dr. Livingstone along with his wife and children. His wife, a daughter of Mr. Moffat, the famous South African missionary, I remember as being a quiet, pleasant-faced, pleasant-spoken woman, and a fit companion for her distinguished husband.

My intercourse with Livingstone did not end with the taking of these photographs. The explorer was anxious to learn photography, with a view to utilising it in his exploration work, and I was only too pleased to show him my process. Photography took a bit of explanation in those days. What with dry plates, ready-made papers, made up developers, roll films, and all other improvements, it has almost ceased to be an art. It has become child's play, and anyone with ordinary care can manipulate a camera, and produce creditable results without any scientific knowledge.

But in those days it was different. I had to make up my collodion with which to coat my plates, had to prepare my own sensitising baths, and had to make my own printing papers. I had to whip up the whites of eggs to get the albumen to coat my papers, and had to dissolve half-crowns in nitric acid to get the nitrate of silver to make them sensitive to light. At that time nitrate of silver was scarcely to be got in the market, and what was could scarcely be depended on for purity. In the same way, when I wanted chloride of gold for toning prints, I had to melt down half-sovereigns with a mixture of nitric acid and hydrochloric acid. These facts show how far we were from the state of advancement which we have now attained.

Livingstone was an apt pupil. His scientific training, of course, stood him in good stead, and he grasped the processes without the least difficulty. He came about my studio a good deal, and I used frequently to dine with him and Mr. Young in Ferguson & Forrester's restaurant in Buchanan Street. At the time a boat was being built for him at the shipyard of Messrs. Tod & Macgregor, and latterly the missionary was fretting at the slow progress that was being made, and which prevented him from getting back to Africa.

Among the more distinguished personages whom I photographed in the course of my career, I may mention Sheriff Alison, whom I remember as a fine, tall, old gentleman, well up in the law. He was an industrious writer as well as a lawyer of distinction, and the author of the voluminous *History of Europe*. Possil House, his residence, where the industrial district of Possilpark now stands, was visited by many of the distinguished literary men and women of the day.

I have also brought my camera to bear on the

broad brow of Sheriff Glassford Bell, the author of that fine poem, "Mary Queen of Scots," which every schoolboy knows by heart.

Gordon Cumming, the African explorer, and a mighty lion-hunter, also faced my camera. He had an exhibition in the Monteith Rooms, Buchanan Street, showing many of the weapons of the natives and skins of the birds and beasts of Africa.

One rather notable gentleman who used to call on me was the Rev. Patrick Brewster, of Paisley Abbey. He was the brother of Sir David Brewster, the well-known optician and inventor of the kaleidoscope. Patrick was more a reformer than a scientist. He was a great opponent of Provost Cochran, of Paisley, and many a fist did they shake at one another in public debate. The soldiers used to attend at the Abbey, and I remember that, while preaching one Sunday, Mr. Brewster denounced the soldiers as a band of hired assassins. The officer in command of the company at once ordered his men to retire, when they all got up in the middle of the sermon and marched out of the church.

I remember Baird of Gartsherrie and Sir Andrew Orr coming to my studio one day. Sir Andrew, who was one of the leading booksellers and stationers in the city, was Lord Provost of Glasgow. After the conclusion of the Crimean war, Sir Andrew Orr and Sandy Baird, as the famous ironmaster was called, went on a tour through the Turkish dominions. On their return home, they called at my studio in Buchanan Street, and were photographed together in Turkish costume. They presented a somewhat strange appearance in the Oriental garb, with turbans and slippers on.

Sandy Baird, although a splendid business man and a very good man in private life—he left half a million to the Church of Scotland—was notoriously deficient in culture. About the time he came to my establishment he was making a collection of books, and while they were waiting for their photographs, they talked about this library. "And do you want the volumes bound in russia or morocco?" queried Sir Andrew Orr. "And what in the world is the sense of sending the books to be bound there," replied Sandy Baird, "when there are plenty of bookbinders at hame?"

I did a good deal of work for Sir Andrew Orr in the way of providing illustrations for some books which he published.

A man of quite a different type was Dr. Norman Macleod of the Barony, one of a famous family of divines, who have done much for the Scottish

Church. A tall, bearded, burly man, with the glow of robust health in his cheeks and a wonderful kindliness of expression in his eye, he looked more like a prosperous farmer than a student and a preacher.

He was a familiar figure in the streets of Glasgow, and might have been seen every Saturday forenoon admiring the fine vessels that thronged the Clyde at the Broomielaw. I knew him well, and used often to sit in his church, which was always crowded. One could not help contrasting his homeliness and the boyish humour, which he showed in conversation or when visiting, with the strong native eloquence, the graphic descriptions, and the earnest appeals which characterised his pulpit utterances.

He was a great friend of the late Queen Victoria, and was frequently called to Balmoral to preach when she went North. But he was not a man to court the favour of the great, and I have heard him tell his congregation to come in their working clothes, so that all classes might attend church on equal terms. I painted a full-sized portrait of him shortly after his return from his tour in India.

Norman Macleod did a great deal of good in Glasgow. He founded the first Congregational Savings Bank in the city, and in one of the busiest centres of labour he started a refreshment-room, where working men could obtain cheap and well-cooked food and enjoy a comfortable reading-room during their meal hours instead of having only the public-houses to go to. He also took a great interest in the administration of the Poor Law, and it was due to his suggestion that pauper children were boarded out with respectable families instead of being herded together in poorhouses.

John Kelso Hunter, named "The Cobbler Artist," was also well known to me. He belonged to the Kilmarnock district, and was a herd in his boyhood days before being apprenticed to the shoemaking business. He worked as a cobbler long after he had begun successfully to paint pictures.

At first he would not do any painting except when the mood was on him, and then he would get up from his cobbler's bench, throw down his tools, take up his brush and palette, which, with his easel, were always at hand, and paint until he felt that the inspiration had left him, and then he would resume his cobbling again.

Latterly, when he had achieved considerably more than a local fame, and commissions were abundant, he gave up the humble business of mending boots, but he retained the *sobriquet*, "The Cobbler Artist" to the last.

He could wield the pen in a trenchant, picturesque manner, and under the *nom de plume* of, I think, "Thomas Turnip," he contributed a number of racy articles dealing with passing events, which appeared in a Glasgow newspaper. One of the best pictures he painted was one of himself working as a cobbler. He showed this in almost every town he visited. He executed a large number of portraits in Ayrshire, as well as in Paisley and towns round about. His charges were not very high, compared with the fees that are now obtained by successful artists.

Kelso Hunter came about my studio, and I had frequent talks with him. I took his portrait, and showed him the process of photography. He was a rough diamond, being a man of no education, but of strongly-marked individuality. I remember him telling me a story of an incident that happened when he was painting a portrait of the Countess of Eglinton. One day he thought that the Countess was looking rather glum, and in order to brighten her up a bit he told her some of his best stories, These anecdotes were perhaps not altogether of the kind that are retailed in drawing-rooms, and the effect was the reverse of what was intended, for the Countess left in high dudgeon. Next day, on going to complete the picture, the cobbler artist found his canvas all cut up with a knife, and a five pound note left on the easel for him. That was a plain hint that his services were no longer required.

When Kelso Hunter published his memoirs he sent me a copy. It is a very interesting volume, written for the most part in the Doric. From it I extract the following interesting paragraph, which explains his interest in the Poet Burns:—

"Nanny Broon and my granny were great companions, and after they were married they were still friends. My mither made her appearance in Maybole in 1768. Nanny Broon came to see the arrival and brought her auld callant alang wi' her. He was nine years old at the time, and the world around Maybole kent him as Robin Burns. The whole world kens him now as Poet Burns. To think that Burns was a callant like me and had herded, planted potatoes, shorn corn, and had done in his day all the drudgery that I was doing in mine, and that he was in Maybole that day my mither was born, and that he had seen her the first day of her existence, and that she had seen him after he was a man, gave the names, the actions, the associations, and the sympathies, the poetry and the love pilgrimage of the poet a home feeling as if he had been an old member of our family."

In another passage Hunter tells how he had been at a New Year dance at Coilsfield in 1827. There he met an old man named Hugh Andrew, sixty-four years of age, who confided to him that he was the "whipper in wee blasted wonner," described by Burns in one of his poems. He also declared that he had danced with Hielan Mary. "Man," he declared, "she was a ticht hizzie."

Among these random recollections I may include another, which the harvest time brings to my mind. The Cross of Glasgow used to be the great place where farmers hired labourers for their harvest operations. Crowds of Irish reapers fresh from the Green Isle were to be seen there of a morning waiting to be hired, each with his hook in his hand. The farmers came down, and picking out the strongest men they could find, took the hooks from those they had hired and marched them off. The rate of pay was generally about 1s. 6d. a day.

In my time I have seen most of the great orators and statesmen, singers, and actors of the last sixty or seventy years. I have listened to the sweet voice of Jenny Lind, and to the rich Irish brogue of Dan O'Connell, the Liberator, to the eloquence of those masters of oratory, Gladstone and Disraeli. I have heard Charles Dickens, the novelist, read from his own works, and have seen and photographed in his younger days Henry Irving, the actor. All these have now crossed the bourne whence no traveller returns, but they live, and will continue to live in my recollections for the sweet and happy emotions which their genius is still able to awaken within me.

## CHAPTER XI.

### MY PHOTOGRAPHIC INVENTIONS.

I HAD my business in Buchanan Street just at the time when that thoroughfare was fast becoming one of the most fashionable in the city. I knew that, as each succeeding term brought a demand for an increase of rent. When I took the attics in 35 Buchanan Street for my engraving business, I was paying the moderate rent of £25 a year. After I started my photographic business and constructed the studio on the roof of my attic, I was, of course, prepared to pay a reasonable increase, but as the landlord saw my business growing immensely, he raised my rent by leaps and bounds, until it stood at £150. Though this was very harassing, I should have been content to pay that figure, but, like Oliver Twist, he still asked for more. He wanted to advance my rent at one bound to £250. This I was not prepared to submit to.

I had concluded an arrangement with the factor of the adjoining property, and had obtained permission to construct a glass house on the roof just adjoining the one I had on No. 35. My factor thought I was just extending my business in the usual way, but he was undeceived when he put forward his demand for an increase of £100 a year on my rent. I told him that I would remove first, and remove I did. I obtained a ten years' lease of the top flat and the glass house at No. 33 at a reasonable figure, and had made communication between the two places, so that when I quitted No. 35 my removal was a simple affair. I was in No. 33 Buchanan Street for many years, and built up a very large business, but I found the same tendency of the rent to go up there. After my lease expired, I had reluctantly to quit Buchanan Street. Then I took rooms at the corner of Jamaica Street and the Broomielaw, on the east side facing Glasgow Bridge. For some years after I quitted my old place in Buchanan Street it stood empty, no one caring to pay so high a rent as was demanded. Then Messrs. Stewart & Macdonald took the building as a workroom for their girls, and subsequently pulled it down, and on its site and on that of their old place put up that enormous warehouse that stands on the corner of Argyll Street and Buchanan Street.

It was while I was in Buchanan Street that I suffered serious loss from an outbreak of fire which took place in the upper stories of my establishment. It was thought to be caused by an escape of gas. A large stock of very valuable negatives was entirely destroyed, a loss which could not be repaired, for many of those whom the photographs represented had crossed the shadowy river, and others had left Glasgow. In this way I lost the negatives I possessed of Dr. Livingstone, Dr. Norman Macleod, Sheriff Glassford Bell, Sheriff Alison, Madeline Smith, and a host of other notabilities.

In the course of my career, I effected some improvements in photography, several of which I patented and worked with considerable profit. The first of these I invented away back in the fifties. I then patented a process of photographing on glass in such a way that figures stood out as they do under the stereoscope. My method was to put the photograph on one side of a plate of glass and to paint in a background on the other. This process proved immensely popular, and I had no difficulty in disposing of as many as I could produce at from one to two guineas each. At the same time, I derived a revenue of £100 a year from a London firm for the right to work the process in the Metropolis. One photographer infringed my patent, but

I went to the Court of Session, and obtained interdict against him. That represented all the trouble I had in connection with this patent.

My most important invention was a machine for printing photographs at a very rapid rate. It was designed to do for photography what the modern printing press has done for printing. I was asked to read a paper before the Glasgow Philosophical Society at the time, describing my printing and developing machines. I did so, and showed them at work printing and developing a number of photographs in the presence of the members. From that paper I give a short description of my invention.

The machine consists of a long box about twelve inches square and of double that length, or may be extended to any size. In a recess in the centre of the box is fitted a pad, over which a band of sixty or seventy feet of sensitised paper passes between the pad and the negative as it rolls from a spool at one end of the box to a drum at the other. Above this pad is a heavy metal frame, with slide to hold the negative, this frame being hinged at one side to admit of its being raised to allow the sensitive paper to move forward at the end of each exposure. Above this frame containing the negative are two gas burners, which are turned down to a peep during the passing of the paper. The light is diffused, and the negative kept cool, by a glass-bottomed trough filled with water interposed between the gas jet and the negative to be printed.

The machine is operated by clockwork. The length of exposure to be given the negative is ascertained, and the machine set for that length of time, any exposure from one second to ten minutes being capable of being registered. The machine can then be set agoing, and it works automatically, requiring no attendant, and doing the work with unfailing accuracy. It turns down the gas and turns it up again for each exposure, winds the exposed part over a drum, and unrolls a fresh length of paper, and registers the number of photos that have been printed. In this way hundreds of copies of one photograph can be thrown off in an hour. I invented a companion machine for developing these spools of photographs quickly.

These inventions I produced in the early eighties, and a company was formed, under the name of the Rapid Photo Printing Company, to exploit them. We had a factory in St. James' Street, Kingston, and for a time we did a considerable business in producing illustrations for book and photographic publishers for engineers' catalogues, etc. But a new invention had been made which was largely to discount the value of mine. The process of photo-engraving had been brought to such a state of perfection that pictures almost equal to actual photographs could be produced in the printing press much more quickly and at much less cost than we could produce ours. Printers' ink is, of course, very much cheaper than bromide of silver, with which we had to coat the paper we used for our photos, and the process or half-tone block had other advantages. We did a big job for the Ilford Company of photographic manufacturers; and soon after the founder of that firm came to Scotland, saw our work, and purchased the patent rights. Though this invention did not prove the great commercial success that I anticipated, I have the satisfaction of knowing that it did something towards bringing about the perfection of the cinematograph.

Before closing these rambling reminiscences, I should like to refer to my greatest hobby—that of angling. Man and boy, I have been a disciple of Isaak Walton for eighty years, and to this no less than to my temperate habits, I ascribe the fact that, during more than seventy years, I have never suffered from a day's illness, or required to dose myself with drugs. I know of no more health-giving pursuit than angling. How delightful it is to tramp over the moors, and through the glens and straths, to the burns and lochs of our native Highlands, leaving all the cares of business behind, and developing a healthy appetite and that weariness that produces sound, refreshing sleep. The memories of fishing forays are amongst the pleasantest of a long life.

I began to use the fishing-rod at an early age. My first angling experience was in connection with the canal at Paisley. My father was an enthusiastic angler, and when I was able to run about I used to get hold of his fishing-basket, and, taking out his gaudiest salmon flies, fixed them on his line, and went and thrashed the dull waters of the canal. Of course I caught nothing, but I saw boys there catching braise by throwing pellets of bread into the water. I asked them what they were fishing with, and they said that it was "cockalindy." I told my father of this, and he burst out, "Oh, the young, poachin' blackguards; they're poisonin' the fish!" It was probably with a view to preserving me from falling into such unsportsmanlike methods that my father agreed to take me with him the next time he went fishing, and thus I was initiated into the noble art of angling long before I was in my "teens." On my first expedition I think we caught some flounders in the Cart. After that I went down to what we called the "water neb," where the Cart runs into the Clyde, and there I caught my first trout. I can remember the triumphant air with which I walked home with my capture. After that I was often down at the "water-neb," sometimes with my fishing-rod and sometimes without it. There was a salmon fishery there, for that lordly fish had not yet forsaken the Clyde. We boys used to assist the fishers to haul in their nets, and were rewarded for our labour with the flounders that were caught, the fishers not troubling with anything less than salmon. There were then numerous salmon fisheries on the Clyde. Besides the one at the "water neb," there was another just where the Co-operative buildings at Shieldhall are, and another in Govan opposite the mouth of the Kelvin. Further down the river there was a fishery at West Ferry opposite Cardross.

I knew Matthew Wallace, who for many years rented the salmon fishery between Renfrew and Port-Glasgow for an annual payment of five pounds. Many a time he gave me an invitation to go down and shoot wild ducks on the mud flats by the river.

In those days also an immense number of eels were caught at the mouth of the Leven for the London market. Every here and there along the banks of the Clyde might be seen the huts of the salmon fishers. The fishing was mostly carried on by weavers, who thus augmented their incomes in the slack season. When the salmon were passing up or down the stream, I have seen from a dozen to a score of fine fish caught in one day.

Since these youthful days I have spent many an hour and day by loch and stream, and lured hundreds of the finny tribe. I am one of the four original members of the St. Mungo Angling Club, one of the oldest organisations of its kind in the city, and, I believe, the largest. It was founded in 1880, and for the first eight years I was president. I am its oldest member, and the roll includes many of the foremost men in the city. I remember some humorous adventures in connection with fishing excursions. On one occasion, a party of us were in a boat fishing. The sport was not very exciting, and my good friend, Professor Dougall, was gazing in an abstracted fashion away to the distant hills. One of the party, noticing this, thought he would take a "rise" out of the professor. He accordingly pulled in the professor's line, fixed a trout he had recently caught on to the professor's hook by the tail, and quietly slipped it overboard. Then he shouted, "Haul in your line, professor. You've got something." Aroused from his reverie, the professor hauled in, and, sure enough, he had a trout, but caught in the most peculiar fashion. Professor Dougall was astonished, but he summoned all his scientific knowledge to his aid in explaining the phenomenon, and we sat with straight faces while he gave us an elaborate disquisition on how such a thing could happen. At the end the practical joker exclaimed, "That's all very well, professor, but you might give me back my fish." The professor, however, had the laugh on his side. He stoutly maintained that his theory was correct, and refused to part with the fish. As the practical joker could not confute his arguments, the trout remained in the professor's basket.

I was the witness of a ludicrous incident while fishing between Tyndrum and Crianlarich. It took place near the dipping pool of St. Fillan, where the witches used to be ducked to get quit of the evil spirit. It was a lovely morning when we were fishing. My friend had put on an artificial minnow, and was fishing up-stream with a long line determined to get a big one, and he did! The Highland

# A Fishing Incident.

cattle were grouped along the banks, adding pictorial beauty to the landscape. All at once I heard a shout, and saw my friend running after one of the cattle, rod in hand. The more he ran the faster the cow made off. At last the brute stopped, and my friend got up, but off the cow bolted again with tail in air. We were convulsed with laughter when one of the party ran after the racing angler and his big catch, flourishing the landing net, and telling him to keep up the point of his rod and give him line, or he would be away with it, and we'd be up with the net to help to land him. At last the angler managed to coax the cow to stand still, and got the hooks of his favourite minnow extracted from its side.

THE END.

# BOOKS

### PUBLISHED BY

## ALEXANDER GARDNER,

### PAISLEY.

Publisher & Bookseller by Special Appointment

To Her late Majesty Queen Victoria.

# A LIST OF BOOKS

PUBLISHED BY

# ALEX. GARDNER, PAISLEY.

*Aitken.*—Love in Its Tenderness. By J. R. Aitken. 3s. 6d.

*Anderson.*—Morison-Grant.—Life, Letters, and Last Poems of Lewis Morison-Grant. By Jessie Annie Anderson. 4s. 6d.

*Anderson.*—Verses at Random. By "Thistle" M. C. Anderson. 2s. 6d. nett.

*Anton.*—The Flywheel: and What Keeps Us Steady. By Rev. Peter Anton. 3s. 6d. nett.

—— Staying Power: Reconsiderations and Recreations. By Rev. Peter Anton. 3s. 6d. nett.

*A. O. M.*—Two Brothers. By A. O. M. 2s. 6d.

*Auld.*—Lyrics of Labour and other Poems. By Thomas C. Auld.

*Ayles.*—Gillicolane. By Grueber Ayles. 4s. 6d.

*Aytoun.*—The Braes o' Balquhidder. By Douglas Aytoun. 6s.

*Ballingal.*—A Prince of Edom. By J. Ballingal, B.D. 2s. 6d.

*Barclay.*—A Renewal in the Church. By Rev. P. Barclay, M.A. 2s. 6d. nett.

*Beatty.*—The Secretar. By W. Beatty. 6s.

—— The Shadow of the Purple. By W. Beatty. 2s. 6d.

"*Belinda's Husband.*"—Plain Papers on Subjects Light and Grave. By "Belinda's Husband." 2s. 6d. nett.

*Beveridge.*—Sma' Folk and Bairn Days. Translated from the Norse by the Rev. John Beveridge, M.A., B.D. 4s. 6d.

*Bilton.*—The Four Gospels. By Ernest Bilton. 2s. 6d.

*Blair.*—The Paisley Thread Industry and the Men who Created and Developed It. By Matthew Blair. 6s. nett.

—— The Paisley Shawl and the Men who Produced It. By Matthew Blair. 7s. 6d. nett.

*Bogatsky.*—A Golden Treasury for the Children of God. By Rev. C. H. V. Bogatsky. Cloth, 2s. Cloth gilt, 2s. 6d.

*Boston.*—A Soliloquy on the Art of Man-Fishing. By Mr. Thomas Boston, A.M. 1s. 6d. nett.

*Brown.*—To Those About to Marry: Dont! Without a Practical Guide. By M. Harriette Brown. 1s. nett.

*Brownlie.*—Hymns of the Holy Eastern Church. Translated by Rev. John Brownlie. 3s. 6d. nett.

────── Hymns from the Greek Office Books: Together with Centos and Suggestions. Translated by Rev. John Brownlie. 3s. 6d. nett.

────── Hymns from the East. Translated by Rev. John Brownlie. 3s. 6d. nett.

*Buchan.*—The Ballad Minstrelsy of Scotland. By Patrick Buchan. 5s.

The Songs of Scotland. Chronologically Arranged. 5s. Uniform with above.

*Bute.*—Coronations — Chiefly Scottish. By the Marquess of Bute, K.T. 7s. 6d. nett.

────── Essays on Foreign Subjects. By the Marquess of Bute, K.T. 10s. 6d.

────── Seven Essays on Christian Greece. Translated by the Marquess of Bute, K.T. 7s. 6d.

*Calder.*—Poems of Life and Work. By Robert H. Calder. 2s. 6d. nett.

*Campbell.*—Notes on the Ecclesiastical Antiquities of Eastwood Parish. By the late Rev. George Campbell. 12s. 6d. and 25s. nett.

*Campbell*—Popular Tales of the West Highlands. By the late J. F. Campbell, Islay. Four vols. 7s. 6d. each.

*Campbell.*—The Elder's Prayer-Book. By Rev. Wm. Campbell, B.D. 1s.

*Carslaw.*—Heroes of the Scottish Covenant. By Rev. W. H. Carslaw, D.D.
      Vol. I.—James Guthrie, of Fenwick.
        II.—Donald Cargill, of the Barony, Glasgow.
        III.—James Renwick, the last of the Martyrs.
1s. 6d. nett each. The three vols. in one, 3s. 6d. nett.

────── Six Martyrs of the First and Second Reformations. By Rev. W. H. Carslaw, D.D. 2s. nett.

*Chalmers.*—Chalmers' Caledonia. 25s. and 40s. per vol. Vol. VIII.—the Index—sold separately, 15s. and 25s. nett.

*Cheviot.*—Proverbs, Proverbial Expressions, and Popular Rhymes of Scotland. By Andrew Cheviot. 6s. nett.

"*Claverhouse.*"—Gretna Green and Its Traditions. By "Claverhouse." 1s. nett.

*Colvin.*—Bell Roger's Loon, and other Stories. By Margaret Colvin. 1s. 6d.

*Cook.*—In a Far Country. By Rev. Thomas Cook, M.A. 3s.

*Craib.*—America and the Americans. By Rev. A. Craib. 3s. 6d.

*Craigie.*—Scandinavian Folk Lore. By W. A. Craigie, M.A., F.S.A. 7s. 6d.

*Crawley-Boevey.*—Beyond Cloudland. By S. M. Crawley-Boevey. 5s.

*Darling.*—Songs from Silence. By Isabella F. Darling. 2s. 6d. nett.

*Downie.*—The Early Home of Richard Cameron. By J. Downie, M.A. 1s. nett.

*Drummond.*—Life of Robert Nicoll. By the late P. R. Drummond, Perth. 5s.

*Edgar.*—Old Church Life in Scotland. By Andrew Edgar, D.D. 7s. 6d.

────── The Bibles of England. By Andrew Edgar, D.D. 7s. 6d.

*Eyre-Todd.*—The Glasgow Poets. Edited by George Eyre-Todd. 7s. 6d. nett.

*Fergusson.*—Alexander Hume. By R. Menzies Fergusson, M.A. 5s. nett.

────── A Student of Nature. By R. Menzies Fergusson, M.A. 4s. nett.

────── A Village Poet. By R. Menzies Fergusson, M.A. 3s. 6d. nett.

────── Rambles in the Far North. By R. Menzies Fergusson, M.A. 3s. and 2s.

*Fergusson.*—Logie: A Parish History. By R. Menzies Fergusson, M.A. 2 vols. 15s. nett. each vol.

—— The Viking's Bride, and other Poems. By R. Menzies Fergusson, M.A. 3s.

*Ferguson.*—The King's Friend. By Dugald Ferguson. 3s. 6d.

*Ferguson.*—The Poems of Robert Ferguson. Edited by Robt. Ford. 5s. nett.

*Fife.*—And I Knew It Not. By David Fife. 3s. 6d. nett.

*Findlay.*—Medici Carmina. By William Findlay, M.D. 3s. 6d. nett.

—— Ayrshire Idylls of Other Days. By "George Umber." 5s.

—— In My City Garden. By "George Umber." 6s.

—— Robert Burns and the Medical Profession. By William Findlay, M.D. ("George Umber.") 6s. nett.

*Fittis.*—Curious Episodes in Scottish History. By R. Scott Fittis. 6s.

—— Heroines of Scotland. By R. Scott Fittis. 6s.

—— Romantic Narratives from Scottish History and Tradition. By R. Scott Fittis. 6s.

*Fleming.*—Ancient Castles and Mansions of Stirling Nobility. By J. S. Fleming, F.S.A. 21s. nett.

*Ford.*—American Humourists. Selected and edited by Robert Ford. 3s. 6d.

—— Auld Scots Ballants. 6s.

—— Ballads of Bairnhood. Selected and edited by Robert Ford. 5s.

—— Ballads of Babyland. Selected and edited by Robert Ford. 5s.

—— Children's Rhymes, Games, Songs, and Stories. By R. Ford. 3s. 6d. nett.

—— Ford's Own Humorous Scotch Stories. 1st and 2nd Series, 1s. each nett. Both Series in 1 vol., 2s. 6d. nett.

—— Poems and Songs of Alexander Rodger. Edited by Robert Ford. 3s. 6d. nett.

—— Tayside Songs and other Verses. By Robert Ford. 3s. 6d. nett.

—— The Harp of Perthshire. Edited by Robert Ford. 15s. and 7s. 6d.

—— Thistledown. By Robert Ford. 3s. 6d. and 1s. nett.

—— Vagabond Songs and Ballads of Scotland. Edited by R. Ford. 5s. nett.

—— Miller's "Willie Winkie," and other Songs and Poems. Edited by Robert Ford. 3s. 6d. nett.

—— The Heroines of Burns. By Robert Ford. 3s. 6d. nett.

—— Popular American Readings. Popular English Readings. Popular Irish Readings, Popular Scotch Readings. Edited by Robert Ford. 1s. each. Also in one vol., 4s.

Gardner's Verse for Schools. Parts I. and II. 6d. nett each part.

*Gentles.*—A Plea for the Restoration of Paisley Abbey. By Rev. T. Gentles, D.D. 1s.

*Gough.*—Scotland in 1298. Edited by Henry Gough. 21s.

—— The Itinerary of King Edward the First, as far as relates to his Expeditions against Scotland, 1286-1307. By Henry Gough. 2 vols. 30s. nett.

*Granger.*—The Average Man, and other Sermons. By the late Rev. William Granger, M.A., Ayr. 3s. 6d. nett.

*Greethead.*—Our Future. Edited by Miss Greethead. 1s. 6d.

*Grey.*—The Misanthrope's Heir. By Cyril Grey. 2s. nett.
*Grosart.*—The Verse and Miscellaneous Prose of Alexander Wilson, the Ornithologist of America. Edited by Rev. A. B. Grosart, LL.D. 12s. 6d.
*Hall.*— The Art of Being Happy. The Art of Being Healthy. The Art of Being Successful. By Rev. Charles A. Hall. 1s. nett each. In one vol., 3s. nett.
*Hall.*—Edith Watson. By Sydney Hall. 3s. 6d.
*Hanton.*—Drifted Northward. By T. Hanton. 1s.
*Harvey.*—Scottish Chapbook Literature. By William Harvey. 3s. 6d. nett.
*Hatherly.*—A Treatise on Byzantine Music. By Rev. S. G. Hatherly, Mus. Bac. (Oxon.). 6s. and 4s.
"God Save the Queen." Supplementary to Dr. Hatherly's Treatise. 2s.
*Henderson.*—Anecdotes and Recollections of A. K. H. B. By Rev. D. R. Henderson, M.A. 6d. nett.
*Henderson.*—Lady Nairne and Her Songs. By Rev. George Henderson, M.A., B.D., Monzie, Crieff. 2s. 6d. nett and 2s. nett.
*Hewat.*—Half-Hours at the Manse. By the Rev. Kirkwood Hewat, M.A., F.S.A. (Scot.), Prestwick. 3s. 6d.
—— In the Olden Times. By Rev. Kirkwood Hewat, M.A., etc. 4s. nett.
Hill-A-Hoy-O. By a "Country Cousin." 2s. 6d.
*Hogg.*—A Tour in the Highlands in 1803. By James Hogg. 2s. 6d.
—— Memoir of James Hogg, the Ettrick Shepherd. By his daughter. 5s.
*Holmes.*—The Teaching of Modern Languages in Schools and Colleges. By D. T. Holmes, B.A. 2s. nett.
*Hume.*—The Practice of Sanctification. By Alexander Hume, B.A. 1s. nett.
*Hutcheson.*—Maisie Warden. By J. D. Hutcheson. 5s.
Isobel Burns (Mrs. Begg). By her Grandson. 2s. 6d.
*James.*—Poems and Fragments. By Charles James. 3s. 6d.
*Jamieson.*—Jamieson's Scottish Dictionary. Edited by David Donaldson, F.E.I.S. 5 vols., £8 17s. 6d.; Large Paper, £14.
—— New Supplementary Volume (being Vol. V. of above). Edited by David Donaldson, F.E.I.S. 27s. 6d. and 42s.
*Johnson.*—A Journey to the Western Islands of Scotland in 1773. By Samuel Johnson, LL.D. New Edition. 2s. 6d. nett.
*Kennedy.*—David Kennedy, the Scottish Singer: Reminiscences of his Life and Work. By Marjory Kennedy. And Singing Round the World: a Narrative of his Colonial Tours. By David Kennedy, Jun. 7s. 6d.
*Kennedy.*—Reminiscences of Walt Whitman. By William Sloane Kennedy, Camden, N.J. 6s.
*Ker.*—Mother Lodge, Kilwinning, "The Ancient Lodge of Scotland." By Rev. W. Lee Ker, Kilwinning. 4s. 6d.
*Kilgour.*—Twenty Years on Ben Nevis. By Wm. T. Kilgour. 2/6 & 1/6 nett.
*Laing.*—The Buke of the Howlat. By Dr. Laing. 12s. 6d.
*Lamont.*—Poems. By J. K. Lamont. 2s. 6d.
*Latto.*—Hew Ainslie: a Pilgrimage to the Land of Burns. Edited by Thomas C. Latto. 6s.

*Latto.*—Memorials of Auld Lang Syne. By Thomas C. Latto. 4s. 6d. and 2s. 6d.
*Law.*—Dreams o' Hame, and other Scotch Poems. By James D. Law. 6s.
*Lumsden.*—Thoughts for Book Lovers. By Harry S. Lumsden. 2s.
*Macbremen.*—Breezes from John o' Groats. By MacBremen. 3s. 6d.
——— The Death of Lady Wallace: a Poem. By MacBremen. 1s.
*M'Cormick.*—Three Lectures on English Literature. By W. S. M'Cormick, M.A. 3s. 6d. nett.
*Macdonald.*—The Husband to Get and to Be. Edited by G. G. Macdonald. 1s. nett.
——— The Wife to Get. 2s. 6d. nett.
*McClelland.*—The Church and Parish of Inchinnan. By the Rev. Robert McClelland, minister of the Parish. 3s. 6d. nett.
*M'Ewen.*—Life Assurance. What to Select. By Robert M'Ewen, Cambus. 3d.
*Macfarlane.*—The Harp of the Scottish Covenant. Poems, Songs, and Ballads collected by John Macfarlane. 6s.
*Macintosh.*—Irvindale Chimes. By John Macintosh. 4s. nett.
——— A Popular Life of Robert Burns. By John Macintosh. 2s. 6d. nett.
*Mackay.*—Where the Heather Grows. By George A. Mackay. 2s. 6d.
*Mackean.*—The King's Quhair. Done into English by Wm. Mackean. 3s. 6d.
*M'Gown.*—Ten Bunyan Talks. By G. W. T. M'Gown. 2s. nett.
——— A Primer of Burns. By G. W. T. M'Gown. 1s. nett.
*M'Kean.*—The Young Naturalists. A Book for Boys and Girls. By Minnie M'Kean. 1st and 2nd Series. 1s. each.
*M'Kellar.*—Greece: Her Hopes and Troubles. By Campbell M'Kellar. 1s.
*M'Kerlie.*—History of the Lands and their Owners in Galloway. By the late P. H. M'Kerlie, F.S.A. Scot., F.R.G.S., etc. 2 vols. 25s. nett.
*MacKenzie.*—History of Kilbarchan Parish. By Robert D. MacKenzie, minister of the Parish. 21s. nett. Large Paper, 35s. nett.
*MacKenzie.*—History of the Outer Hebrides. By William C. MacKenzie. 12s. 6d. nett. Large Paper, 21s.
——— The Lady of Hirta. By Wm. C. MacKenzie, F.S.A. Scot. 6s.
——— A Short History of the Scottish Highlands and Isles. By Wm. C. MacKenzie. New Edition. 5s. nett.
*Macleod.*—Wallace: a Poem. By Neil Macleod. 1s., post free.
*McMillan.*—Mainly About Robert Bruce. By Alec McMillan, M.A. 1s. nett.
*Mackintosh.*—The History of Civilisation in Scotland. By John Mackintosh, LL.D. 4 vols. £4 4s. Calf Extra, £5 5s. Large Paper, £6 6s.
*MacNicol.*—Dare MacDonald. By E. R. MacNicol. 5s.
*Macpherson.*—History of the Church in Scotland. By Rev. John Macpherson, M.A. 7s. 6d.
*Macrae.*—A Feast of Fun. By Rev. David Macrae. 3s. 6d.
——— Book of Blunders. By Rev. David Macrae. 1s.
——— National Humour. By Rev. David Macrae. 3s. 6d.
——— The Railway Chase, and other Sketches. By Rev. David Macrae. 1s.
——— Popping the Question, and other Sketches. By Rev. David Macrae. 1s. The above two volumes in one, 2s.

*Mather.*—Poems. By James Mather. 4s.
——— Poems. Second Series. By James Mather. 5s. nett.
*Maughan.*—Rosneath: Past and Present. By W. C. Maughan. 5s.
——— The Garelochside. By W. C. Maughan. 7s. 6d.
——— Picturesque Musselburgh and Its Golf Links. By W. C. Maughan. Cloth, 1s. 6d. Paper covers, 1s. nett.
*Menzies.*—Illustrated Guide to the Vale of Yarrow. By James M. Menzies. 1s. 6d. nett.
*Menzies.*—National Religion. By Rev. Allan Menzies, D.D., St. Andrews. 5s.
*Menzies.*—Provincial Sketches and other Verses. By G. K. Menzies. 2s. 6d. nett.
*Metcalfe.*—SS. Ninian and Machor—the Legends of, in the Scottish Dialect of the Fourteenth Century. By W. M. Metcalfe, D.D. 10s. 6d. nett. On Whatman Paper, 15s. nett.
——— A History of the Shire of Renfrew from the Earliest Times down to the Close of the Nineteenth Century. By W. M. Metcalfe, D.D., F.S.A. 25s. nett. On Whatman Paper, 40s.
——— Charters and Documents relating to the Burgh of Paisley. By W. M. Metcalfe, D.D. 21s. nett.
——— Ancient Lives of the Scottish Saints. Translated by W. M. Metcalfe, D.D. 15s. On Whatman Paper, 25s.
——— Pinkerton's Lives of the Scottish Saints. Revised and enlarged by W. M. Metcalfe, D.D. 2 vols. 15s. per vol.
——— The Natural Truth of Christianity. Edited by W. M. Metcalfe, D.D. 5s.
——— The Reasonableness of Christianity. By W. M. Metcalfe, D.D. 5s.
*Metcalfe.*—The Great Palace of Constantinople. Translated from the Greek of Dr. A. G. Paspates, by William Metcalfe, B.D. 10s. 6d.
*Miller.*—Selections from the Works of Hugh Miller. Edited by W. M. Mackenzie, M.A., F.S.A. (Scot.). 3s. 6d.
*Mitchell.*—A Popular History of the Highlands and Gaelic Scotland. By Dugald Mitchell, M.D., J.P. 12s. 6d. nett.
*Mitchell.*—Jephtha: a Drama. Translated by A. G. Mitchell. 3s. 6d. nett.
——— John the Baptist: a Drama. Translated by A. G. Mitchell. 3s. 6d. nett.
*Morison-Grant.*—Protomantis, and other Poems. By L. Morison-Grant. 6s.
*Motherwell.*—Poems and Songs. By William Motherwell. 6s.
*Mowat.*—Search Light. By G. H. Mowat. 2s. 6d. nett.
*Munro.*—Burns' Highland Mary. By Archibald Munro. 3s.
*Munro.*—Schleiermacher. By Robt. Munro, B.D., Old Kilpatrick. 4s. 6d. nett.
*Murray.*—A Handbook of Psychology. By J. Clark Murray, LL.D., F.R.S.C., M'Gill College, Montreal. 7s. 6d.
——— An Introduction to Ethics. By J. Clark Murray, LL.D., etc. 6s. 6d.
——— A Sketch of the Life and Times of the late David Murray, Esq., Provost of Paisley. By his son, J. Clark Murray, LL.D., etc. 4s.
——— Solomon Maimon. Translated by J. Clark Murray, LL.D., etc. 6s.
*Murray.*—Kilmacolm: a Parish History. By Rev. Jas. Murray, M.A. 6s. nett.
——— Life in Scotland a Hundred Years Ago. By Rev. James Murray, M.A. Second and Enlarged Edition. 3s. 6d. nett.

*Murray.*—The Black Book of Paisley and other Manuscripts of the Scotichronicon. By David Murray, LL.D., F.S.A., Scot. 12s. 6d.
*Mursell.*—The Waggon and the Star. By Walter A. Mursell. 2s. 6d. nett.
*Naismith.*—The Young Draper's Guide to Success. By W. Naismith. 1/6 nett.
*Nicoll.*— Warp and Woof : Hesps of Homespun Yarns. By David M. Nicoll. 1s. Cloth, 1s. 6d.
*Nicolson.*—Tales of Thule. By John Nicolson. 2s.
*Ochiltree.*—Redburn. By Henry Ochiltree. 5s.
On Heather Hills. 2 vols. 21s.
*Paton.*—Honouring God. By Rev. James A. Paton, M.A. 4s. 6d.
——— Balmanno : a Study in Social Regeneration. By Rev. James A. Paton, D.D. 1s. 6d. Paper Covers, 1s.
*Patterson.*—The "Cyclops" of Euripides. Edited by John Patterson, B.A. (Harvard), Louisville, Kentucky, U.S.A. 4s. 6d.
*Perin.*—Divine Breathings. By Christopher Perin. 1s.
*Phelps.*—The Still Hour. By Rev. Austen Phelps. 6d.
*Phillips.*—Cora Linn. By J. G. Phillips. 3s. 6d., post free.
——— James Macpherson, the Highland Freebooter. By J. G. Phillips. 3s. 6d.
*Philp.*—The River and the City. By Rev. George Philp, Glasgow. 6d.
*Rae-Brown.*—The Shadow on the Manse. By Campbell Rae-Brown. 3s. 6d.
*Reid.*—A Cameronian Apostle. By Professor Reid, D.D. 6s.
*Reid.*—Poems, Songs, and Sonnets. By Robert Reid (Rob Wanlock). 5s.
*Reid.*—Problems of this Life—Social and Sacred. By W. Reid. 2s. 6d. nett.
Renfrewshire. Archæological and Historical Survey of the County, under the direction of several eminent antiquaries. Lochwinnoch. With numerous Plates. 2 vols. 25s. per vol. Large Paper, 37s. 6d.
Renfrewshire—Geographical and Historical. 3d.
*Renwick.*—Poems and Sonnets. By James Renwick. 2s. 6d.
*Rigg.*—Nature Lyrics. By James Rigg. 2s. 6d. nett.
*Roberts.*—A Short Proof that Greek was the Language of Christ. By the late Professor Roberts, D.D., St. Andrews. 2s. 6d.
*Robertson.*—Jockie, and other Songs and Ballads. By A. S. Robertson. 1s. 6d.
*Robertson.*—Practical First Aid. By Wm. Robertson, M.D., D.P.H. 1s. 6d. nett.
——— The Stone of Dunalter. By Wm. Robertson, M.D., D.P.H. 3s. 6d.
*Robertson.*—The Lords of Cuningham. By Wm. Robertson. 5s.
*Ross.*—Highland Mary. Edited by John D. Ross. 2s. 6d.
——— Random Sketches on Scottish Subjects. By John D. Ross. 2s. 6d.
——— Round Burns' Grave. The Paeans and Dirges of Many Bards. Gathered together by John D. Ross. 3s. 6d.
*Ross.*—In the Highlands, and other Poems. By G. R. T. Ross. 3s. 6d. nett.
*Ross.*—Kingcraft in Scotland. By Peter Ross, LL.D. 6s.
*Roy.*—Lilias Carment ; or, For Better for Worse. By Gordon Roy. 6s.
*Russell.*—Three Years in Shetland. By Rev. John Russell, M.A. 3s. 6d.
Scotland Eighty Years Ago. Thirty-two Fine Copperplate Etchings of the Chief Towns and their Surroundings. £5 5s. to subscribers only.

*Scott.*—Lectures for Club and Cloister. By A. Boyd Scott. 3s. 6d. nett.
*Seath.*—Rhymes and Lyrics. By Wm. Seath. 3s. 6d. nett.
Silver Aims and Golden Anchors. A Text-Book. 1s. nett.
*Simpson.*—Familiar Scottish Birds. By A. Nicol Simpson, F.Z.S. 2s.
——— Familiar Scottish Animals. By A. Nicol Simpson, F.Z.S. 2s.
——— Bobbie Guthrie: a Scotch Laddie. By A. N. Simpson, F.Z.S. 2s. 6d. nett.
*Skinner.*—That Loon o' Baxter's. By Rev. J. Skinner. 2s.
*Smith.*—Scottish Athletic Sports. By W. M'Combie Smith. 1s. 6d.
*Smith.*—The Dalbroom Folks. By Rev. J. Smith, M.A., B.D. 2 vols. 6s.
*Smith.*—The New Testament in Braid Scots. Rendered by Rev. Wm. Wye Smith. New Edition. 6s. nett.
*Snodgrass.*—Wit, Wisdom, and Pathos, from the Prose of Heinrich Heine. Selected and translated by J. Snodgrass. 6s.
*Stephen.*—Divine and Human Influence. By Rev. R. Stephen, M.A. 5s. nett.
*Stewart.*—The Church of Scotland. By Richard Morris Stewart. 7s. 6d.
*Story.*—Health Haunts of the Riviera and South-West of France. By Very Rev. Principal Story, D.D. 3s.
——— St. Modan of Rosneath. By the Very Rev. Principal Story, D.D. 2s.
*Sturrock.*—Our Present Hope and Our Future Home. By Rev. J. B. Sturrock. 2s. 6d. nett.
*Sutherland.*—The Selected Works of Robert Burns. Edited by Rhona Sutherland. Crown 4to. 430 pp. With Illustrations. Price 5s. nett. Or in various Bindings—Prices on application.
*Symington.*—Hints to Our Boys. By A. J. Symington. 1s. 6d.
*Tannahill.*—Poems and Songs of Robert Tannahill. Edited by the late David Semple, F.S.A. New Edition. 3s. 6d. nett.
*Taylor.*—The Autobiography of Peter Taylor. 3s. 6d.
*Taylor.*—Twelve Favourite Hymns: their Messages and their Writers. By Rev. Wm. Taylor, M.A. 2s. nett.
The Knight of Snowdon; or, The Saxon and the Gael. 2s. 6d.
The Leading Aisles: Volume One. 2s. 6d.
*Tweeddale.*—Dunty the Droll. By John Tweeddale. 1s.
*Urie.*—Reminiscences of 80 Years. By John Urie.
*Veitch.*—The Dean's Daughter. By Sophie F. F. Veitch. 3s. 6d.
*Warrick.*—The History of Old Cumnock. By Rev. John Warrick, M.A., Free Church, Old Cumnock. 7s. 6d. nett.
*Watt.*—Selected Metrical Psalms and Paraphrases. Selected and edited by R. MacLean Watt, M.A., B.D. 1s. nett.
*Whyte.*—Naigheachdan Firinneach (True Stories). Vol. I. Translated into Gaelic by Henry Whyte ("Fionn"). 3s. 6d. nett. Vol. II. in the Press.
*Mac-Choinnich.*—Eachdraidh a' Phrionnsa; no, Bliadhna Thearlaich (The Jacobite Rising of 1745). Le Iain Mac-Choinnich. New Edition. 5s. nett.
*Williamson.*—Cartsburn and Cartsdyke. By G. Williamson. 25s. and 42s.
——— Old Greenock. Second Series. Uniform with above.
*Wright.*—Laird Nicoll's Kitchen, and other Sketches of Scottish Life and Manners. By Joseph Wright. 2s. 6d. nett.
*Young.*—Scotch Cameos. By John Young. New Edition, 1s. and 1s. 6d.

## MANUALS FOR THE HOUSEHOLD.

Cookery for Working Men's Wives. By Martha H. Gordon. 1d.; post free, 2d. Large Type Edition, 3d.; post free, 4d.
Indigestion. By Florence Stacpoole. 2d.; post free, 2½d.
Our Babies, and How to Take Care of Them. By Florence Stacpoole. 3d.; post free, 4d.
The Home Doctor. By Florence Stacpoole. 3d.; post free, 4½d.

## THE "JENNY WREN" SERIES. 6d. each. Post free, 8d.

A Treatise on the Cooking of Big Joints.
Dainty Dishes for Dinners, Luncheons, and Suppers.
Dishes of Fishes: How to Prepare Them.
Sauces, Seasonings, and Salads.
The Art of Preparing Puddings, Tarts, Jellies, etc.
The Art of Preparing Soups, Stews, Hashes, and Ragouts.
The Complete Art of Dinner-Giving.

www.ingramcontent.com/pod-product-compliance
Lightning Source LLC
LaVergne TN
LVHW061214060426
835507LV00016B/1932